10

MINUTE GUIDE TO

POWERPOINT® 97

by Faithe Wempen

que®

A Division of Macmillan Computer Publishing
201 West 103rd St., Indianapolis, Indiana 46290 USA

To Margaret

© **1996 by Que® Corporation**

International Standard Book Number: 0-7897-1021-8

Library of Congress Catalog Card Number: 96-7145-0

98 97 96   8 7 6 5 4 3 2 1

Interpretation of the printing code: the rightmost number of the first series of numbers is the year of the book's printing; the rightmost number of the second series of numbers is the number of the book's printing. For example, a printing code of 96-1 shows that the first printing of the book occurred in 1996.

Printed in the United States of America.

Publisher Roland Elgey

Editorial Services Director Elizabeth Keaffaber

Managing Editor Michael Cunningham

Senior Product Development Specialist Lorna Gentry

Product Development Specialist John Gosney

Production Editor Linda Seifert

Copy Editors Patricia A. Solberg and Mike McFeely

Cover Designer Dan Armstrong

Designer Glenn Larsen

Indexer Rebecca Hornyak

Production Janelle Herber, Lori Price, Chris Morris

Special thanks to Nanci Jacobs for ensuring the technical accuracy of this book.

CONTENTS

INTRODUCTION

Congratulations on choosing Microsoft PowerPoint 97! PowerPoint is one of the most powerful and flexible business-presentation programs sold today. Whether you need to create some simple text overheads for a speech at a local club, or a high-impact animated show for an important business deal, PowerPoint can handle the job.

Although PowerPoint comes with many features to help the beginner, it's still not a simple program. You probably won't be able to dive right in without instructions. But you certainly don't want to wade through a 500-page manual to find your way around!

- You want a clear-cut, plain-English introduction to PowerPoint.

- You need to create a professional-looking, usable presentation—fast.

- You don't have much time to study graphic-design theory.

You need the *10 Minute Guide to PowerPoint 97*.

WHAT IS MICROSOFT POWERPOINT 97?

Microsoft PowerPoint 97 is a graphics program designed for use with Microsoft Windows 95, Windows NT Workstation 3.51, or Windows NT 4.0. PowerPoint 97 specializes in creating effective business presentations. Many graphics programs can help you draw, but PowerPoint can help you put text and drawings, colors and shapes together to effectively convey a message.

What Is Windows 95? Windows 95 is a powerful 32-bit operating system for desktop PCs. To use Microsoft PowerPoint 97, you have to have Windows 95, Windows NT Workstation 3.51, or Windows NT 4.0 loaded on your PC. There are other versions of PowerPoint for other operating systems, such as Windows 3.x (16-bit versions of the Windows operating system) and the Apple Macintosh.

Here are just a few things you can do with PowerPoint:

- Type the text for a presentation directly into PowerPoint, or import it from another program.

- Set a consistent, readable color scheme and layout for your entire presentation, or custom-design each slide.

- Create dazzling animations and transitions between slides which you can control with a few keystrokes as you give the presentation. No more fumbling with transparencies!

- Create audience handouts and speaker's notes that supplement your presentation.

- Show others your presentation on-screen, in printed form, or on the Internet.

You'll learn to do all of this and more in this book.

Installing PowerPoint If you purchased PowerPoint as part of the Microsoft Office 97 suite, you probably already installed it when you installed the suite. If you haven't installed Microsoft PowerPoint on your computer, see the inside front cover of this book for instructions.

What is the *10 Minute Guide?*

The *10 Minute Guide* series is a quick approach to learning computer programs. Instead of trying to cover the entire program, the *10 Minute Guide* teaches you only about the features of PowerPoint that a beginner is most likely to need.

No matter what your professional demands, the *10 Minute Guide to PowerPoint 97* will help you find and learn the main features of the program and become productive with it more quickly. You can learn this wonderfully logical and powerful program in a fraction of the time you would normally spend learning a new program.

Conventions Used in This Book

Each of the lessons in this book include step-by-step instructions for performing a specific task. The following icons will help you identify particular types of information:

 Timesaver Tips   These offer shortcuts and hints for using the program most effectively.

 Plain English   These identify new terms and definitions.

 Panic Button   These appear in places where new users often run into trouble.

Specific conventions in this book help you to easily find your way around Microsoft PowerPoint:

What you type	appears in **bold, color** type.
What you select	appears in color type.
Menu, Field, and Key names	appear with the first letter capitalized.

ACKNOWLEDGMENTS

Thanks to the wonderful editors of the Que New Users Group who tackled this project with me at such a busy time in their schedule: Lorna Gentry, John Gosney, and Linda Seifert. Their conscientious work and attention to detail made this book a pleasure to work on.

And closer to home, thanks to my chosen family for keeping me fed and sane when I got into a writing frenzy: Margaret for making home-cooked meals every night, Jane for dropping off garlic bagels on her way to work, Chuck for letting me blow off steam about my projects, and the Cheap Nylons softball team ("a run every time!"), especially Sam and Donna, for always keeping the cooler packed with cold ones. The Bleacher Babe says "Hey."

TRADEMARKS

All terms mentioned in this book that are known to be trademarks have been appropriately capitalized. Que Corporation cannot attest to the accuracy of this information. Use of a term in this book should not be regarded as affecting the validity of any trademark or service mark.

STARTING AND EXITING POWERPOINT

In this lesson, you will learn how to start and exit PowerPoint.

STARTING POWERPOINT

Before you start PowerPoint, you must have PowerPoint installed on your computer, and you should have a basic understanding of the Windows 95 or Windows NT operating systems. If you need a refresher course in these Windows systems, read the "The Windows Primer" at the back of this book. Throughout this book, I'll be referring to Windows 95, but keep in mind that in most cases, if you're using Windows NT, the information applies to you too.

To start PowerPoint, follow these steps:

1. Click the Start button.

2. Move your mouse pointer to Programs. A menu of programs appears.

3. Move your mouse pointer to Microsoft PowerPoint and click on it (see Figure 1.1). PowerPoint starts and displays the introductory screen shown in Figure 1.2.

The first thing you see when you start PowerPoint is a dialog box in which you choose whether you want to start a new presentation or open an existing one. You'll learn about this dialog box in Lesson 2. For now, click Cancel to exit this dialog box.

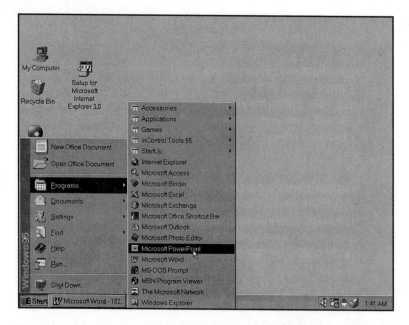

FIGURE 1.1 To start PowerPoint, move through the Start button's menu system to Microsoft PowerPoint.

 PowerPoint Not On the Menu? You may have specified a different menu when you installed PowerPoint, or you may not have installed PowerPoint yet.

 Help! There's a Paper Clip Talking to Me! No, you haven't lost your mind. That paper clip is one of Microsoft Office's Assistants. Occasionally the little guy gives you a suggestion, and you have to click the appropriate button below his words to move on. The first time you start PowerPoint, he might say something. Clicking the Close button (X) for his window or pressing Esc will enable you to continue with your work. We'll look at the Office Assistants more in Lesson 4.

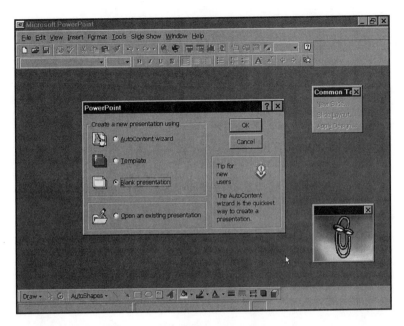

FIGURE 1.2   When you first start PowerPoint, you see an introductory dialog box. (You'll learn about it in Lesson 2.)

EXITING POWERPOINT

When you finish using PowerPoint, you should exit. Don't just turn off your computer!

To exit PowerPoint:

1. If the PowerPoint dialog box is still on-screen, click the Cancel button to close it.

2. If this dialog box is not on-screen, do one of the following (see Figure 1.3):

   - Click the PowerPoint window's Close (X) button.

   - Double-click on the Control-menu icon in the left corner of the title bar, or click it once to open the Control-menu and then select Close.

   - Open the File menu and select Exit.

   - Press Alt+F4.

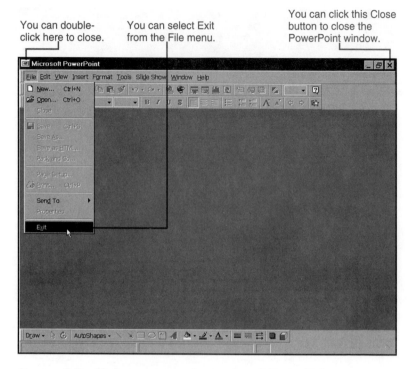

You can double-click here to close.

You can select Exit from the File menu.

You can click this Close button to close the PowerPoint window.

FIGURE 1.3 There are several ways to exit PowerPoint.

3. If you're asked if you want to save your changes, select Yes to save your changes. (If you choose Yes, see Lesson 6 to learn how to complete the Save As dialog box that appears.) Select No if you haven't created anything you want to save yet.

In this lesson, you learned to start and exit PowerPoint. In the next lesson, you'll learn how to create a new presentation.

CREATING A NEW PRESENTATION

In this lesson, you will learn how to create a presentation in several different ways.

THREE CHOICES FOR STARTING A NEW PRESENTATION

PowerPoint offers you several ways to create a new presentation. Before you begin, decide on the method that's right for you:

- AutoContent Wizard offers the highest degree of help. It walks you through each step of creating the new presentation.

- A template offers a standardized group of slides, all with a similar look and feel, for a particular situation. Each template slide includes dummy text which you can replace with your own text.

- You can choose to start from scratch and create a totally blank presentation, but building the presentation from the ground up is not recommended for beginners.

 Wizards Wizards are a special feature that most Microsoft products offer. A wizard displays a series of dialog boxes that ask you design and content questions. You select options and type text. When you are done, the Wizard creates something (in this case, a presentation) according to your instructions.

Template A template is a predesigned slide that comes with PowerPoint. When you select a template, PowerPoint applies the color scheme and general layout of the slide to each slide in the presentation.

A WORD ABOUT THE POWERPOINT DIALOG BOX

If you have just started PowerPoint and the PowerPoint dialog box is displayed, you are ready to start a new presentation (see Figure 2.1). From here, you can choose to create a new presentation using the AutoContent Wizard, a Template, or a Blank Presentation. Just click on your choice, then click OK, and follow along with the steps in the remainder of this lesson to complete the presentation.

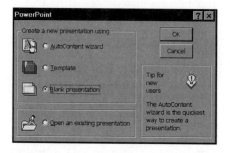

FIGURE 2.1 When you first start PowerPoint, this dialog box greets you. It's one method you can use to create a new presentation.

Unfortunately, this dialog box is available only when you first start the program. Once you close the dialog box, you won't see it again until the next time you start the program. That's why the steps in the remainder of this lesson don't rely on it; instead they show alternative methods for starting a presentation if this dialog box is not available.

CREATING A NEW PRESENTATION WITH THE AUTOCONTENT WIZARD

With the AutoContent Wizard, you select the type of presentation you want to create (strategy, sales, training, reporting, conveying bad news, or general) and PowerPoint creates an outline for the presentation. Here's how you use the AutoContent Wizard:

Quick Start   You can click the AutoContent Wizard button in the PowerPoint dialog box shown in Figure 2.1 then click OK, and then skip the first three steps in the following procedure.

1. Open the File menu and click New. The New Presentation dialog box appears.

2. Click the Presentations tab if it's not already on top. (See Figure 2.2.)

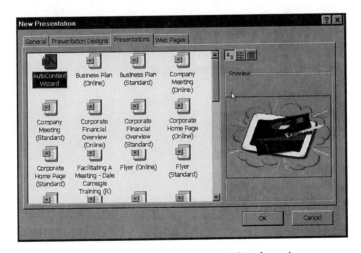

FIGURE 2.2   You can start a new presentation from here.

3. Double-click the AutoContent Wizard icon. The AutoContent Wizard starts.

Macro Warning   At step 3, you may get a warning message about macros possibly carrying viruses. Just click Enable Macros to continue.

4. Click the Next button to begin.

5. In the dialog box that appears (see Figure 2.3), click the button that best represents the type of presentation you want to create (for example, Sales/Marketing).

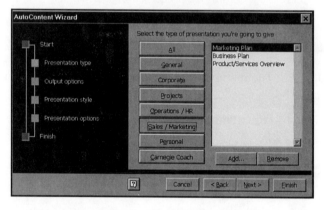

FIGURE 2.3   Just answer the AutoContent Wizard's questions and click Next.

6. Click on a presentation on the list that further narrows your presentation's purpose (for example, Marketing Plan). Then click Next.

7. Choose the method that best describes how you will give the presentation:

- **Presentations, informal meetings, handouts** Choose this if you are planning the presentation with a live narrator controlling the action.

- **Internet, kiosk** Choose this if you are planning a self-running presentation that does not require a live narrator.

8. Click Next to continue.

9. Choose the type of output you need (I'm choosing On-screen presentation), and whether you need handouts (Yes or No). Then click Next.

10. Enter the presentation title and your name in the blanks provided. Then click Next.

11. Click Finish. The beginnings of your presentation, with dummy text in place, appear on-screen in Outline view. (You'll learn about Outline view, as well as other views, in Lesson 5.)

 TIP   **Replacing Dummy Text**   You can start personalizing your presentation right away by replacing the dummy text with your own text. Just select the existing text and type right over it. See Lesson 11 for more information about editing text.

CREATING A NEW PRESENTATION WITH A TEMPLATE

A template is the middle ground between maximum hand-holding (the AutoContent Wizard) and no help at all (Blank Presentation). There are two kinds of templates: Presentation Templates and Presentation Design Templates:

- **Presentation Templates**   These templates offer much of the same help as the AutoContent Wizard—in fact, the AutoContent Wizard bases its presentation types on these. The templates provide a color scheme for slides and a basic outline for slide text. Their names reflect the purpose of the presentation, for example, "Communicating Bad News."

- **Presentation Design Templates**   These templates offer only a color scheme and a "look" for slides—you're on your own to provide the content for each slide.

To start a new presentation using a template, follow these steps:

1. Open the File menu and select New. The New dialog box opens.

2. If you want to use a Presentation Template, click the Presentations tab. If you want to use a Presentation Design, click the Presentation Designs tab.

3. Click on the template you want to use. A preview of the template appears in the Preview area.

4. After you select the template you want to use, click OK. PowerPoint creates the new presentation based on that template.

5. If you have selected a Presentation Template, you are ready to start editing the slides, just like with the AutoContent Wizard. If you have selected a Presentation Design Template, you see the New Slide dialog box (see Figure 2.4). Click on the AutoLayout you want to use, and click OK.

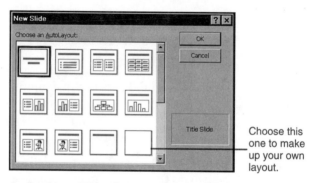

Choose this one to make up your own layout.

FIGURE 2.4   In the New Slide dialog box, you can choose a predesigned slide layout, or you can choose to design your own.

>
>
> **The Next Step?**   To start customizing a Presentation Template, just click on the dummy text and type new text to replace it. You can work through the whole presentation that way—the upcoming lessons, especially Lesson 11, can help.
>
> To customize a Presentation Design Template, just add more slides by clicking on the New Slide button on the toolbar and create your presentation one slide at a time. See Lesson 9 for help.

CREATING A BLANK PRESENTATION

Are you sure you want to attempt a blank presentation on your first time out? A blank presentation has no preset color scheme or design, and no dummy text to help you know what to write. To create a blank presentation, follow these steps:

1. Open the File menu and select New.

2. Click the General tab.

3. Double-click the Blank Presentation icon. The New Slide dialog box appears (refer to Figure 2.4).

4. Select the AutoLayout you want to use, click on it, and click OK.

WHAT'S NEXT?

Now you have the basic shell of your presentation, but you need to modify and customize it. If you're not in a hurry, I suggest reading the lessons in this book in order so you can learn PowerPoint fully. However, if you're in a hurry, refer to the following lessons:

- To change the view of the presentation so you can work with it more easily, see Lesson 5, "Working with Slides in Different Views."

- To apply a different design template or slide layout, see Lesson 8, "Changing a Presentation's Look."

- To add new slides, see Lesson 9, "Inserting, Deleting, and Copying Slides."

- To rearrange slides, see Lesson 10, "Rearranging Slides in a Presentation."

- To add and edit text, see Lesson 11, "Adding Text to a Slide."

In this lesson, you learned how to create a new presentation. In the next lesson, you will learn how to control the PowerPoint program with menus and toolbars.

GETTING AROUND IN POWERPOINT

In this lesson, you will learn how to get around in PowerPoint and enter commands.

A LOOK AT POWERPOINT'S APPLICATION WINDOW

If you created a new presentation using the AutoContent Wizard or a template, your screen looks something like the screen shown in Figure 3.1. This screen contains many of the same elements you find in any Windows 95 or Windows NT program: a title bar, window control buttons (Minimize, Maximize, and Close), and a menu bar. For an explanation of these elements, refer to the "The Windows Primer" at the back of this book.

In addition, you see three toolbars and several windows that are unique to PowerPoint. The following sections explain how to work with these unique items.

Toolbar A toolbar is a collection of buttons that enables you to bypass the menu system. For example, instead of selecting File, Save (opening the File menu and selecting Save), you can click the Save toolbar button to save your work. (You'll learn more about saving in Lesson 6.)

Turning Off the Office Assistant The Office Assistant provides help as you work. If you don't want the Office Assistant on-screen all the time, you can easily make it disappear. Just click the Close (X) button on its window. To make it reappear, select Help, Microsoft PowerPoint Help. You'll learn more about the Office Assistant in Lesson 4.

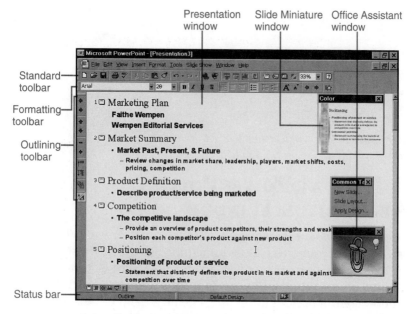

FIGURE 3.1   PowerPoint provides many tools for quickly entering commands.

New to PowerPoint 97   is the Common Tasks window, shown in Figure 3.1. This is actually a floating toolbar. (You'll learn about floating toolbars later in this lesson.) You can drag it around on the screen, or get rid of it completely by clicking its Close (X) button. You can get it back by right-clicking any toolbar and selcting Common Tasks from the shortcut menu.

THE PRESENTATION WINDOW

In the center of the PowerPoint window is a presentation window. (It's probably maximized, so it flows seamlessly into the larger PowerPoint window.) You use this window to create your slides and arrange them into a presentation. At the bottom of the presentation window are several buttons that enable you to change views. Figure 3.1 shows a presentation in Outline view, whereas Figure 3.2 shows the same presentation in Slide view. For details about changing views, see Lesson 5.

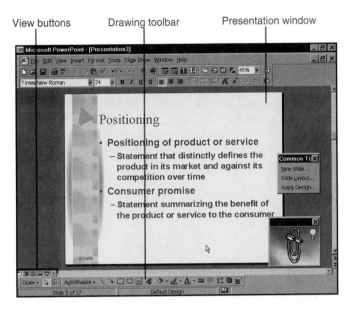

View buttons   Drawing toolbar   Presentation window

FIGURE 3.2 You can change views by simply clicking on a View button.

Slide Miniature Window? Slide Miniature is a new feature in PowerPoint 97. It enables you to view a small version of a slide even in nongraphical views like the one shown in Figure 3.1. You'll learn more about it in Lesson 5, "Working with Slides in Different Views."

USING SHORTCUT MENUS

Although you can enter all commands in PowerPoint using menus, PowerPoint offers a quicker way: context-sensitive shortcut menus like the ones in Windows 95 and Windows NT. To use a shortcut menu, move the mouse pointer over the object you want the command to act on, and then click the right mouse button. A shortcut menu pops up (as shown in Figure 3.3), offering commands that pertain to the selected object. Click on the desired command.

I right-clicked here
to display the menu.

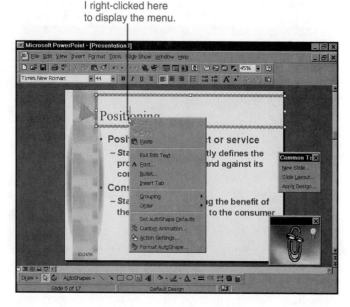

FIGURE 3.3   Display a shortcut menu by right-clicking on the object.

WORKING WITH TOOLBARS

PowerPoint displays three toolbars by default: the Standard and Formatting toolbars below the menu bar (see Figure 3.1) and either the Outlining toolbar (on the left) or the Drawing toolbar (on the bottom), depending on the view. To select a button from the toolbar, just click on the button.

PowerPoint on the Web   There is also a Web toolbar that you can use to browse the World Wide Web through PowerPoint. It isn't turned on by default, but you can activate it by right-clicking on any toolbar and selecting Web, as you'll learn later in this lesson.

LEARNING MORE ABOUT TOOLBAR BUTTONS

Although I could list and explain all the tools in the Standard toolbar and in all the other toolbars, here are some better ways to learn about the buttons:

- **To see the name of a button**, move the mouse pointer over the button. PowerPoint displays a ScreenTip that provides the name of the button.

- **To learn more about a button,** press Shift+F1 or select Help, What's This? and then click on the button for which you want more information.

TURNING TOOLBARS ON OR OFF

If you never use a particular toolbar, you can turn it off to free up some screen space. In addition, you can turn on other toolbars that come with PowerPoint but don't appear automatically. To turn a toolbar on or off:

1. Right-click on any toolbar. A shortcut menu appears (see Figure 3.4). A check mark appears beside each toolbar that is turned on.

2. Click on the displayed toolbar you want to hide, or click on a hidden toolbar that you want to display. Check marks appear beside displayed toolbars.

FIGURE 3.4 The shortcut menu for toolbars displays the names of all the toolbars.

When you click on a toolbar name on the menu, the menu disappears and that toolbar appears (if it was hidden) or the toolbar disappears (if it was displayed).

Moving Toolbars

After you have displayed the toolbars you need, you can position them in your work area wherever they are most convenient. Here's how to move a toolbar:

1. Position the mouse pointer at the far left edge of the toolbar.

2. Hold down the left mouse button, and drag the toolbar where you want it according to these guidelines:

   - Drag the toolbar to a toolbar dock. There are four docks: just below the menu bar, on the left and right sides of the application window, and just above the status bar.
   - Drag the toolbar anywhere else inside the application window to create a floating toolbar (see Figure 3.5).

 Toolbar Dock A toolbar dock is a location on the screen where a toolbar can "blend in" and meld with the PowerPoint window, rather than floating in its own separate box. By default, the Standard and Formatting toolbars are docked at the top and the Drawing toolbar is docked at the bottom.

3. Release the mouse button.

 What About Drop-Down Lists? If a toolbar contains a drop-down list, you cannot drag it to the left or right toolbar dock.

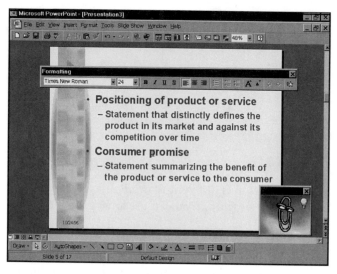

FIGURE 3.5   A floating toolbar.

A floating toolbar acts just like a window. You can drag its title bar to move it or drag a border to size it. If you drag a floating toolbar to a toolbar dock, the toolbar turns back into a normal (nonfloating) toolbar.

TIP   **Customizing a Toolbar**   To customize a toolbar, right-click on it and choose Customize. You can then drag a toolbar button from one toolbar to another or drag a button off a toolbar (to remove it). To add a button, click the Commands tab in the Customize dialog box, and select a feature category from the Categories list in the dialog box. Then drag the desired command to any of the toolbars to create a button for it.

In this lesson, you learned about the PowerPoint application and presentation windows, and you learned how to enter commands with shortcut menus and toolbars. In the next lesson, you learn how to use the PowerPoint Help system.

GETTING HELP

In this lesson, you'll learn about the various types of help available to you in PowerPoint.

HELP: WHAT'S AVAILABLE?

Because every person is different, PowerPoint offers many ways to get help with the program. You can use any of these methods to get help:

- Ask the Office Assistant for help.

- Choose what you're interested in learning about from a series of Help topics.

- Get help on a particular element you see on-screen with the What's This? tool.

ASKING THE OFFICE ASSISTANT

You have probably already met the Office Assistant; it's the paperclip character that pops up to give you advice. Don't let its whimsical appearance fool you, though; behind the Office Assistant is a very powerful Help system.

Upgrade Tip The Office Assistant replaces the Answer Wizard feature found in PowerPoint for Windows 95.

TURNING THE OFFICE ASSISTANT ON OR OFF

By default, the Office Assistant is turned on, and sits in a little box on top of whatever you're working on, as shown in Figure 4.1. You can turn it off by clicking the Close (X) button in its top right corner.

FIGURE 4.1 The Office Assistant appears in its own window, on top of the PowerPoint window.

To turn the Office Assistant on again, click the Office Assistant button in the Standard toolbar or select Help, Microsoft PowerPoint Help.

THE KINDS OF HELP OFFICE ASSISTANT PROVIDES

When you first turn on the Office Assistant, a bubble appears next to (or above) its box asking you what kind of help you want (see Figure 4.2). You can do any of the following:

- Type a question in the text box provided to tell the Office Assistant what kind of help you need. (More on this shortly.)

- Select one of the Office Assistant's "guesses" about what you need help with.

- Click the Tips button to get any tips that the Office Assistant can provide for the task you're performing.

- Click the Options button to customize the way the Office Assistant works. (I'll explain more about this later in this lesson.)

- Click Close to close the bubble (but leave the Office Assistant on-screen).

If you close the help bubble, you can reopen it at any time by clicking the Help button on the Standard toolbar, pressing F1, or selecting Help, Microsoft PowerPoint Help, or clicking on the Office Assistant window.

Figure 4.2 Office Assistant at your service, asking what you need help with.

TIP

Extra Tips Along the Way Sometimes you'll see a light bulb next to the Office Assistant in its window. This means that the Office Assistant has a suggestion for you regarding the task that you're currently performing. To get the suggestion, just click the light bulb. Click the Close button when you're finished reading the suggestion.

ASKING THE OFFICE ASSISTANT A QUESTION

If you need help on a particular topic, simply type a question into the text box shown in Figure 4.2. Follow these steps:

1. If the Office Assistant's help bubble doesn't appear, click the Help button on the Standard toolbar.

2. Type a question into the text box. For instance, you might type **How do I save?** to get help saving your work.

3. Click the Search button. The Office Assistant provides some topics that might match what you're looking for. For instance, Figure 4.3 shows the Office Assistant's answer to the question "How do I save?"

FIGURE 4.3 The Office Assistant asks you to narrow exactly what you are trying to accomplish, so it can provide the best help possible.

4. Click on the option that best describes what you're trying to do. For example, I'm going to choose **Save a presentation** from Figure 4.3. A Help window appears with instructions for the specified task.

   If none of the options describe what you want, click the See more arrow to view more options, or type in a different question in the text box.

The Help window that appears that contains the task instructions is part of the same Help system that you can access with the Help, Contents and Index command. See "Managing Help Topics You've Located" later in this lesson for information about navigating this window.

USING THE POWERPOINT HELP TOPICS

A more conventional way to get help is through the Contents and Index command on the Help menu. When you open the PowerPoint Help system this way, you move through the topics listed to find the topic in which you're interested.

There are several tabs in the Help system, so you can use Help the way you want. To access the Help system:

1. Select Help, Contents and Index.

2. Click on the tab for the type of help you want (explained in the next sections).

3. Click on the topic in which you're interested, if there's a list, or type in your topic and press Enter.

The following sections contain specific information about each tab.

CONTENTS

The Contents tab of the Help system is a series of "books" you can open. Each book has one or more Help topics in it, and some books contain sub-books! Figure 4.4 shows a Contents screen.

To select a Help topic from the Contents screen, follow these steps:

1. Select Help, Contents and Index.

2. Click the Contents tab.

3. Find the book that describes, in broad terms, what you're looking for help with.

4. Double-click on the book. A list of Help topics appears below the book, as shown in Figure 4.4.

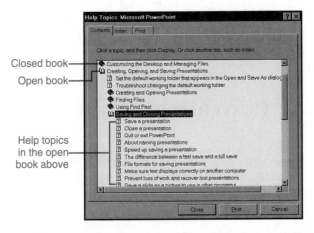

FIGURE 4.4 The Help Contents screen is a group of books that contain Help information.

5. Double-click on a Help topic to display it.

INDEX

The Index is an alphabetical listing of every Help topic available. It's like an index in a book. To use the Index, follow these steps:

1. Select Help, Contents and Index.

2. Click the Index tab.

3. Type the first few letters of the topic you want to find. The index list jumps quickly to that spot (see Figure 4.5).

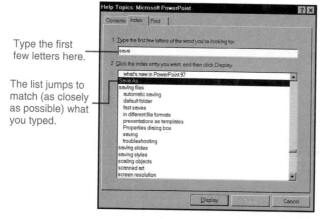

Type the first few letters here.

The list jumps to match (as closely as possible) what you typed.

FIGURE 4.5 Browse through topics alphabetically with the Index.

4. When you find the topic you want, double-click on the topic.

FIND

The Index is great if you know the name of the Help topic that you are looking for, but what if you're not sure? That's where Find comes in handy. Find searches not only the titles of help topics, but their contents, and retrieves all the topics in which the word(s) you typed appear.

To use Find, follow these steps:

1. Select Help, Contents and Index.

2. Click the Find tab.

3. If This is the first time you've used Find, the Find Setup Wizard appears. Click Next, then Finish to move through it. Otherwise, go on to the next step.

4. Type the topic you're looking for in the top box.

5. If more than one line appears in the middle box, click on the one that most closely matches your interest.

6. Browse through the topics that appear in the bottom box, and click on the one that matches the help you need (see Figure 4.6).

7. Click the Display button or press Enter.

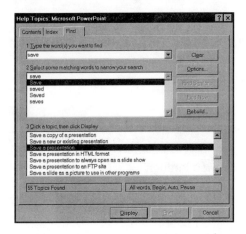

FIGURE 4.6 Use Find to locate all the Help topics that deal with a certain subject.

MANAGING HELP TOPICS YOU'VE LOCATED

No matter which of the four avenues you choose for finding a help topic (the Office Assistant, Contents, Index, or Find), you eventually end up at a Help screen of instructions like the one shown in Figure 4.7. From here, you can read the information on-screen or do any of the following:

- Click an underlined word to see a definition of it.

- Click a button to jump to another Help screen. For example, in Figure 4.7, a >> button is available to take you to a screen of related information.

- Print a hard copy of the information by clicking the Options button and then selecting Print Topic.

- Copy the text to the Clipboard (for pasting into a program such as Microsoft Word or Windows Notepad) by clicking the Options button and then selecting Copy.

- Return to the previous Help topic you viewed by clicking the Back button. If you have not looked at other Help topics this session, the Back button is not available.

- Return to the main Help Topics screen by clicking the Help Topics button.

- Close the Help window by clicking the Close (X) button.

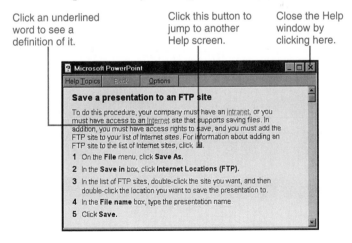

FIGURE 4.7 Once you arrive at the information you need, you can read it on-screen, print it, or move to another Help topic.

GETTING HELP WITH SCREEN ELEMENTS

If you wonder what a particular button or tool on the screen is used for, wonder no more. Just follow these steps:

1. Select Help, What's This?

2. Click on the screen element for which you want help. A box appears explaining the element.

In this lesson, you learned about the many ways that PowerPoint offers help. In the next lesson, you'll learn about the different views PowerPoint offers for working with your presentation.

WORKING WITH SLIDES IN DIFFERENT VIEWS

In this lesson, you will learn how to display a presentation in different views and to edit slides in Outline and Slide views.

CHANGING VIEWS

PowerPoint can display your presentation in different views. Having the option of selecting a view makes it easier to perform certain tasks. For example, Outline view shows the overall organization of the presentation, whereas Slide Sorter view enables you to quickly rearrange the slides. Figure 5.1 shows the available views.

To change views, open the View menu and choose the desired view: Slide, Outline, Slide Sorter, or Notes Pages. A quicker way to switch views is to click the button for the desired view at the bottom of the presentation window, as shown in Figure 5.2.

Outline to Slide View If you're using Outline view, you can quickly display a slide in Slide view by double-clicking on the desired slide icon in the outline.

What About the Slide Show Button? No, I haven't forgotten the Slide Show button. It enables you to view your presentation as a timed slide show. For details, see Lesson 22.

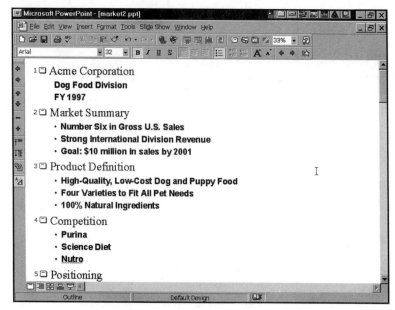

FIGURE 5.1   You can change views to make a task easier.

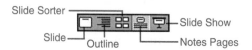

FIGURE 5.2   Use these buttons to change views.

MOVING FROM SLIDE TO SLIDE

When you have more than one slide in your presentation, you will need to move from one slide to the next to work with a specific slide. The procedure for selecting a slide depends on which view you are currently using:

- In Outline view, use the scroll bar to display the slide you want to work with. Click on the Slide icon (the icon to the left of the slide's title) to select the slide, or click anywhere inside the text to edit it.

- In Slide view or Notes Pages view, click on the Previous Slide or Next Slide button just below the vertical scroll bar (as shown in Figure 5.3), or drag the box inside the scroll bar until the desired slide number is displayed, or press Page Up or Page Down.

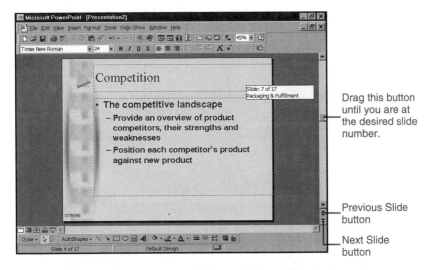

Drag this button until you are at the desired slide number.

Previous Slide button

Next Slide button

FIGURE 5.3   Use the Previous Slide and Next Slide buttons to move between slides in Slide or Notes Pages view.

- In Slide Sorter view, click on the desired slide. A thick border appears around the selected slide.

THE SLIDE MINIATURE WINDOW

The Slide Miniature window is a new feature in PowerPoint 97 (see Figure 5.4). When it's turned on, it displays the currently selected slide in a small window on top of whatever view you're using.

To turn Slide Miniature on or off, select View, Slide Miniature.

In Outline view, the Slide Miniature shows a color version of the selected slide. In all other views, it shows an alternate version of the slide. For example, if you are currently displaying the slides on-screen in color, the Slide Miniature window shows them in black-and-white. Conversely, if the slides are displayed in black-and-white, the Slide Miniature window shows them in color.

The Slide Miniature window is especially useful if you are developing a presentation for two different media—for example, an on-screen presentation and a black-and-white set of printouts. Slide

Miniature helps you keep an eye on the look of the slides so you do not inadvertently make a change to a color slide, for example, that would make it look unattractive or illegible when printed in black-and-white.

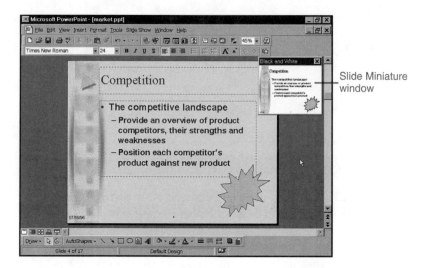

Slide Miniature window

FIGURE 5.4 The Slide Miniature window provides a thumbnail sketch of the current slide.

 TIP **Color or Black-and-White?** To toggle between Black and White and Color views on-screen, open the View menu and select Black and White (if you're currently viewing color) or Color (if you're currently viewing black-and-white).

EDITING SLIDES

If you created a presentation in Lesson 2 using the AutoContent Wizard or a template, you already have several slides, but they may not contain the text you want to use. If you created a blank presentation, you have one slide on the screen that you can edit.

In the following sections, you will learn how to edit text in Outline and Slide views. In later lessons, you will learn how to add and edit text objects, pictures, graphs, organizational charts, and other items.

 Object   An object is any item on a slide, including text, graphics, and charts.

EDITING TEXT IN OUTLINE VIEW

Outline view provides the easiest way to edit text (see Figure 5.5). You simply click to move the insertion point where you want it, and then type in your text. Press the Del key to delete characters to the right of the insertion point or the Backspace key to delete characters to the left.

To select text, hold down the left mouse button and drag the mouse pointer over the desired text. You can then press the Del or Backspace key to delete the text, or you can drag the text where you want to move it.

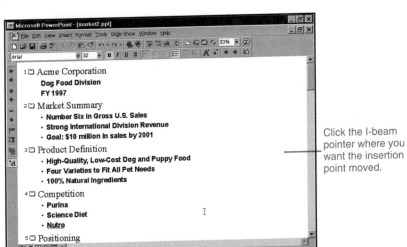

Click the I-beam pointer where you want the insertion point moved.

FIGURE 5.5   Switch to Outline view to edit text.

Auto Word Select   When you select text, PowerPoint selects whole words. If you want to select individual characters, open the Tools menu, select Options, click the Edit tab, and select Automatic Word Selection to turn it off. Click the OK button.

CHANGING THE TEXT'S OUTLINE LEVEL

As you can see from Figure 5.5, your presentation is organized in a multilevel outline format. The slides are at the top level of the outline, and each slide's contents are subordinate under that slide. Some slides have multiple levels of subordination (for example, a bulleted list within a bulleted list).

You can easily change an object's level in Outline view with the Tab key:

- Click on the text, then press the Tab key or click the Demote button on the Outlining toolbar to demote it one level in the outline.

- Click on the text, then press Shift+Tab or click the Promote button on the Outlining toolbar to promote it one level in the outline.

In most cases, subordinate items on a slide appear as items in a bulleted list. In Lesson 12, you will learn how to change the appearance of the bullet, and the size and formatting of text for each entry, as well as how much the text is indented for each level.

MOVING A LINE IN OUTLINE VIEW

As you work in Outline view you may find that some paragraphs need to be rearranged. One easy way is with the Move Up and Move Down buttons on the Outlining toolbar.

• To move a paragraph up in the outline, select it, then click the Move Up button.

 • To move a paragraph down in the outline, select it, then click the Move Down button.

 Dragging Paragraphs You can quickly change the position or level of a paragraph by dragging it up, down, left, or right. To drag a paragraph, move the mouse pointer to the left side of the paragraph until the pointer turns into a four-headed arrow. Then hold down the left mouse button and drag the paragraph to the desired position.

Editing in Slide View

Slide view provides an easy way to edit all objects on a slide, including text and graphic objects. As shown in Figure 5.6, you can edit an object by clicking or double-clicking on it. For a text object, click on the object to select it, and then click where you want the insertion point moved. For a graphic object, double-click on it to bring up a set of tools that will help you edit it.

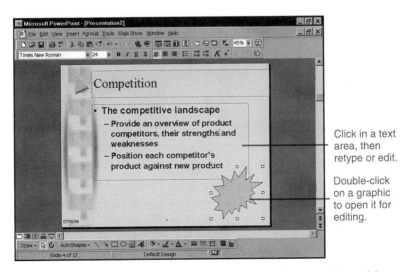

Figure 5.6 Slide view enables you to edit both text and graphic objects.

Most text appears on the slide in text boxes. (The only other place text can appear is within a graphic object.) In Lesson 11, you'll learn more about adding text to a slide, including creating your own text boxes on a slide. Then in Lessons 12 and 13 you'll learn how to fine-tune the look of your text for maximum impact.

Editing graphics is a more tricky than editing text. Lessons 14 and 15 discuss placing graphics on slides, and Lessons 19 and 20 cover manipulating graphics.

In this lesson, you learned how to change views for a presentation, move from slide to slide, and edit text. In the next lesson, you'll learn how to save, close, and open a presentation.

Saving, Closing, and Opening Presentations

In this lesson, you will learn how to save a presentation to disk, close a presentation, and open an existing presentation.

Saving a Presentation

Soon after creating a presentation, you should save it on disk to protect the work you have already done. To save a presentation for the first time, follow these steps:

1. Select File, Save, or press Ctrl+S, or click the Save button on the Standard toolbar. The Save dialog box appears.

2. In the File name text box, type the name you want to assign to the presentation. Do not type a file extension; PowerPoint automatically adds the extension .PPT (see Figure 6.1).

 Upgrade Tip Because PowerPoint 97 is a 32-bit application, you are not limited to the old 8-character file names, as you were with PowerPoint versions designed for Windows 3.x. Your file names can be as long as you like (within reason—the limit is 255 characters) and can include spaces.

3. The Save In box shows which folder the file will be saved in. The default is My Documents. If you want to save to a different drive or folder, see the next section in this lesson. Otherwise, continue to step 4.

4. Click Save.

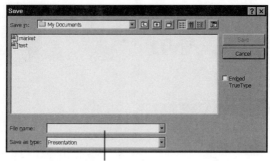

Type the file name here.

FIGURE 6.1   The Save dialog box.

Now that you have named the file and saved it to a disk, you can save any changes you make simply by pressing Ctrl+S or clicking the Save button on the Standard toolbar. Your data is saved under the file name you assigned.

To create a copy of a presentation under a different name, select File, Save As. The Save As dialog box appears, and you can use it in the same way you did when you originally saved the file.

CHANGING THE DRIVE OR FOLDER

The dialog boxes for opening and saving files in Windows 95 are different from the ones in Windows 3.1. The Save As and Open dialog boxes take a bit of getting used to.

To change to a different drive, you must open the Save In or Look In drop-down list. (The name changes depending on whether you're saving or opening a file.) Figure 6.2 shows this drop-down list in the Open dialog box. From it, choose the drive on which you want to save the file.

Next, you must select the folder where you want to save the file (or open it from). When you select the drive, a list of the folders on that drive appears. Double-click on the folder you want to select.

Table 6.1 explains the buttons and other controls you see in the Save As and Open dialog boxes, as well as in other Windows 95 dialog boxes you might encounter.

Select the drive from this list.

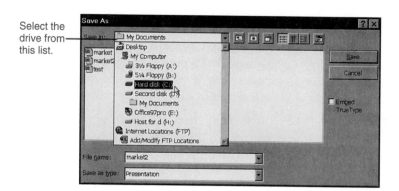

FIGURE 6.2   Use this drop-down list to choose a different drive.

TABLE 6.1   BUTTONS FOR CHANGING DRIVES AND FOLDERS IN WINDOWS 95 DIALOG BOXES

CONTROL	PURPOSE
	Moves to the folder "above" the one shown in the Save In box (that is, the folder in which the current one resides).
	Shows the C:\WINDOWS\FAVORITES folder, no matter which folder was displayed before.
	Creates a new folder.
	Shows the folders and files in the currently displayed folder in a list.
	Shows details about each file and folder.
	Shows the properties of each file and folder.
	Opens a dialog box of settings you can change that affect the dialog box.

continues

TABLE 6.1 CONTINUED

	(Appears in Open dialog box only.) Switches to Preview view, in which you can see the first slide of a presentation before you open it.
	(Appears in Open dialog box only.) Adds a shortcut to the currently displayed folder to the Favorites list.

CLOSING A PRESENTATION

You can close a presentation at any time. If you are working on multiple presentations, it's alright to keep them all open at once, but the more presentations you have open, the slower PowerPoint's response time to your commands will be, so you should close any presentations that you are not working on.

Note that although this closes the presentation window, it does not exit PowerPoint. To close a presentation, follow these steps:

1. If more than one presentation is open, open the Window menu and select the one you want to close.

2. Choose File, Close, press Ctrl+F4, or click the Close (X) button. If you have not saved the presentation, or if you haven't saved since you made changes, a dialog box appears asking if you want to save.

3. To save your changes, click Yes. If this is a new presentation, refer to the steps earlier in this lesson for saving a presentation. If you have saved the file previously, the presentation window closes.

OPENING A PRESENTATION

Once you save a presentation to a disk, you can open the presentation and continue working on it at any time. Follow these steps:

1. Choose File, Open, or press Ctrl+O, or click the Open button on the Standard toolbar. The Open dialog box appears (see Figure 6.3).

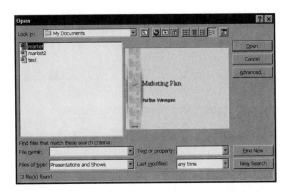

FIGURE 6.3   Select the presentation you want to open.

2. If the file isn't in the currently displayed folder, change drives and/or folders. Refer to "Changing the Drive or Folder," earlier in this lesson.

3. Double-click on the file to open it.

 Files From Other Programs?   You can open files from some other presentation programs in PowerPoint, such as Harvard Graphics. For information about this, see Lesson 27, "Exchanging Data."

FINDING A PRESENTATION FILE

If you're having trouble locating your file, PowerPoint can help you look. Follow these steps to find a file:

1. Choose File, Open if the Open dialog box is not already open.

2. In the File Name box at the bottom of the dialog box, type the name of the file you're looking for. (Refer to Figure 6.3.)

Wild Cards   You can use wild cards if you don't know the entire name of a file. The asterisk (*) wild-card character stands in for any character or set of characters, and the question mark (?) wild-card character stands in for any single character. For example, if you know the file begins with P, you could type P*.ppt to find all PowerPoint files that begin with P.

3. (Optional) Enter other search criteria:

   - If you're looking for a different file type, choose it from the Files of Type drop-down list.

   - If you're looking for a file containing certain text, type that text in the Text or Property box.

   - If you know when you last modified the file, choose the time interval from the Last Modified drop-down list.

4. Click the Advanced button. The Advanced Find dialog box appears (see Figure 6.4).

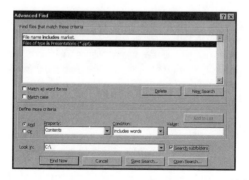

FIGURE 6.4   Use the Advanced Find dialog box to select the folders and drives you want to search.

5. In the Look In section at the bottom of the Advanced Find dialog box, narrow the search area as much as possible using these techniques:

- If you are sure the file is in a certain folder, type that folder's path (such as C:\WINDOWS) in the Look In box.

- If you are sure the file is on a certain drive, select that drive from the Look In drop-down list.

- If you don't know which drive contains the file, select My Computer from the Look In drop-down list.

6. Make sure the Search Subfolders check box is marked. If it isn't, click on it.

7. Click the Find Now button. The File Open dialog box reappears and displays the files that match your search criteria.

8. Double-click on the desired file to open it.

 TIP **More Search Options** As you may have noticed in Figure 6.4, there are a lot more complex search options available—too many to cover here. See your PowerPoint documentation for more details.

In this lesson, you learned how to save, close, open, and find presentations. In the next lesson, you will learn how to print a presentation.

PRINTING PRESENTATIONS, NOTES, AND HANDOUTS

In this lesson, you will learn how to select a size and orientation for the slides in your presentation and how to print the slides, notes, and handouts you create.

Notes and Handouts For instructions on how to create audience handouts and speaker's notes, see Lessons 23 and 24.

QUICK PRINTING—NO OPTIONS

The quickest way to print is to use all the default settings. You don't get to make any decisions about your output, but you do get your printout without delay.

To print a quick copy, follow any of these steps:

- Click the Print button on the Standard toolbar.
- Choose File, Print, and click the OK button.
- Press Ctrl+P, and click the OK button.

When you use these methods for printing, you get a printout of your entire presentation in whatever view is on-screen. The following list describes what type of printout you can expect from each view.

- **Slide view** The entire presentation prints in Landscape orientation. Each slide fills an entire page.

- **Outline view**   The entire outline prints in Portrait orientation.

- **Slide Sorter view**   The entire presentation prints in Portrait orientation with six slides per page.

- **Notes Pages view**   The entire presentation prints in Portrait orientation with one slide per page. Each slide prints with its notes beneath it.

Orientation   The orientation setting tells the printer which edge of the paper should be at the "top" of the printout. If the top is across the wide edge, it's Landscape; if the top is across the narrow edge, it's Portrait.

CHANGING THE SLIDE SETUP

If you didn't get the printouts you expected from the previous procedure, you can change the selected presentation output, size, and orientation of the presentation in the Page Setup dialog box. To customize your printouts, follow these steps:

1. Choose File, Page Setup. The Page Setup dialog box appears on-screen, as shown in Figure 7.1.

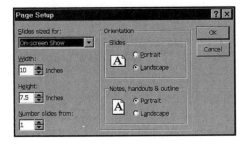

FIGURE 7.1   The Page Setup dialog box enables you to set the position and size of the slides on the page when you print them in Slide view.

2. Perform one of the following procedures to set the slide size:

   • To use a standard size, select a size from the Slides Sized For drop-down list. For example, you can have slides sized for regular 8.5 × 11 paper, 35mm slides, or an on-screen slide show.

   • To create a custom size, enter the dimensions in the Width and Height text boxes.

Spin Boxes   The arrows to the right of the Width and Height text boxes enable you to adjust the settings in those boxes. Click on the up arrow to increase the setting by .1 inch, or on the down arrow to decrease it by .1 inch.

3. In the Number Slides From text box, type the number with which you want to start numbering slides. (This is usually 1, but you may want to start with a different number if the presentation is a continuation of another.)

4. Under the Slides heading, choose Portrait or Landscape orientation for your slides.

5. In the Notes, Handouts & Outline section, choose Portrait or Landscape for those items.

Can I Print Notes and Handouts Differently?   If you want your notes printed in portrait orientation and your handouts printed in landscape orientation, just choose Portrait from the Notes, Handouts & Outline section of the Page Setup dialog box and print the notes. Then, before you print the handouts, go back to this dialog box and choose Landscape from the Notes, Handouts & Outline section.

6. Click OK. If you changed the orientation of your slides, you may have to wait a moment while PowerPoint repositions the slides.

Choosing What and How to Print

If the default print options don't suit you, you can change them. Do you have more than one printer? If so, you can choose which printer to use. For example, you may want to use a color printer for overhead transparencies and a black-and-white printer for your handouts. You can also select options for printing multiple copies and for printing specific slides only.

To set your print options, follow these steps, and then print.

1. Choose File, Print. The Print dialog box appears, with the name of the currently selected printer in the Name box (see Figure 7.2).

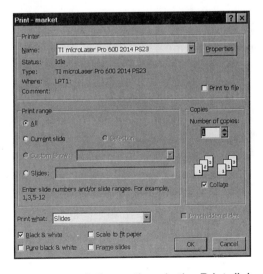

Figure 7.2   Choose your printing options in the Print dialog box.

2. If you want to use a printer different from the one that appears, open the Name drop-down list and select a different printer.

Printer Properties To make adjustments to your printer's settings, click on the Properties button in the Print dialog box. The adjustments you can make vary from printer to printer, but you should be able to adjust graphics quality, select paper size, and choose which paper tray to use, among other things.

3. Choose what to print in the Print Range section:

- Choose All to print all the slides in the presentation.

- Choose Current Slide to print only the currently displayed slide.

- Enter a range of slide numbers in the Slides text box—for example, **2-4** to print slides 2, 3, and 4.

4. Open the Print What drop-down list and choose what you want to print. You can print slides, handouts, notes, or outlines.

5. If you want more than one copy, enter the number of copies you want in the Number of Copies box.

6. Select or deselect any of these check boxes in the dialog box as desired:

Print to File Select this option to send the output to a file rather than to your printer.

Collate If you are printing more than one copy, select this check box to collate (1, 2, 3, 1, 2, 3) each printed copy instead of printing all the copies of each page at once (1, 1, 2, 2, 3, 3).

Black & White If you have a black and white printer, select this check box to make the color slides print more crisply. You also can select this check box to force a color printer to produce black-and-white output.

Pure Black & White   This check box is like the preceding one except everything prints in solid black and plain white, with no grey shading. This makes all slides look like line drawings.

Scale to Fit Paper   If the slide (or whatever you're printing) is too large to fit on the page, select this check box to decrease the size of the slide to make it fit on the page. Now you won't have to paste two pieces of paper together to see the whole slide.

Frame Slides   Select this check box if you want to print a border around each slide.

Print Hidden Slides   If you have any hidden slides, you can choose whether to print them. If you don't have any hidden slides, this check box will be unavailable. You'll learn about hidden slides in Lesson 10.

TIP

Why Would I Print to File?   If you don't have the printer that you want to use hooked up to your computer, you can print to a file, and then take that file to the computer where the printer is. The other computer does not need to have PowerPoint installed on it to print PowerPoint documents.

7. Click OK to print.

In this lesson, you learned how to print slides, outlines, and notes, and how to set options for your printouts. In the next lesson, you will learn how to change the overall appearance of the slides in a presentation.

CHANGING A PRESENTATION'S LOOK

In this lesson, you will learn various ways to give your presentation a professional and consistent look.

GIVING YOUR SLIDES A PROFESSIONAL LOOK

PowerPoint comes with dozens of professionally designed slides you can use as templates for your own presentations. That is, you can apply one of these predesigned slides to an already existing presentation to give the slides in your presentation a consistent look.

Template A template is a predesigned slide that comes with PowerPoint. When you select a template, PowerPoint applies the color scheme and general layout of the slide to each slide in your presentation.

There's another way to make global changes to the entire presentation: you can alter the Slide Master. The Slide Master is not really a slide, but it looks like one. It's a design grid that you make changes on; these changes affect every slide in the presentation. For example, if you want a graphic to appear on every slide, you can place it on the Slide Master instead of pasting it onto each slide individually. When you apply a template, you are actually applying that template to the Slide Master, which in turn applies the template's formatting to each slide.

Changing the Colors on a Single Slide If you want to make some slides in the presentation look different from the others, you're in the wrong lesson. Check out Lesson 17 to learn how to apply different color schemes to individual slides.

APPLYING A PRESENTATION DESIGN TEMPLATE

You can apply a different template to your presentation at any time, no matter how you originally create your presentation. To change the template, follow these steps:

1. Click the Apply Design button on the Standard toolbar, or choose Format, Apply Design. The Apply Design dialog box appears (see Figure 8.1).

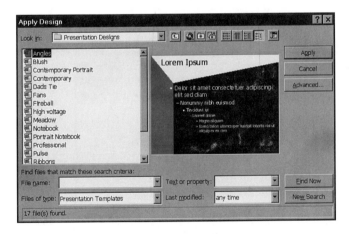

FIGURE 8.1   Choose a different template from the Apply Design dialog box.

2. Click on a template name in the Name list. A sample of the template appears to the right of the list.

3. When you find a template you want to use, click Apply.

USING AUTOLAYOUTS

While templates enable you to change the color and design of a presentation, AutoLayouts enable you to set the structure of a single slide in a presentation. For example, if you want a graph and a picture on a slide, you can choose an AutoLayout that positions the two items for you.

 TIP   **Individual Slides?**   PowerPoint applies AutoLayouts to individual slides, but the template you choose and the Master Layout modifications you make affect the AutoLayouts. This becomes more evident later in this lesson.

To use an AutoLayout, do the following:

1. In Slide view, display the slide you want to change.

2. Choose Format, Slide Layout. The Slide Layout dialog box appears (see Figure 8.2).

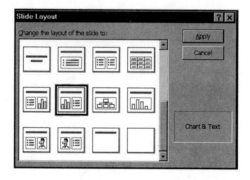

FIGURE 8.2   You can change an individual slide's layout with this dialog box.

 TIP   **Right-Click**   A quick way to display the Slide Layout dialog box is to right-click on the slide in Slide view and select Slide Layout.

3. Click on the desired layout, or use the arrow keys to move the selection border to it.

4. Click on the Apply button. PowerPoint applies the selected layout to the current slide.

EDITING THE SLIDE MASTER

Every presentation has a Slide Master that controls the overall appearance and layout of each slide. The Slide Master contains all the formatting information that the template brings to the presentation, such as colors and background patterns, and it also marks where the elements you use from the AutoLayout feature will appear on the slide.

To make changes to the Slide Master for your presentation, follow these steps:

1. Select View, Master, Slide Master. Your Slide Master appears, as in Figure 8.3.

2. Make any changes to the Slide Master, as you'll learn in upcoming lessons in this book. (Anything you can do to a regular slide, you can do to a Slide Master.)

3. When you're done working with the Slide Master, click the Close button (see Figure 8.3) to return to normal view.

The two most important elements on the Slide Master are the Title Area and Object Area for the AutoLayout objects. The Title Area contains the formatting specifications for each slide's title; that is, it tells PowerPoint the type size, style, and color to use for the text in the title of each slide. The Object Area contains the formatting specifications for all remaining text on the slide.

Slide Miniature   As you learned in Lesson 5, Slide Miniature is a new viewing tool in PowerPoint 97. It enables you to see what the slide will look like in another format (for example, in black-and-white if the slide is currently shown in color). Turn back to Lesson 5 for more information.

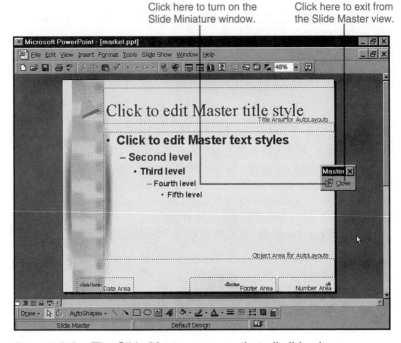

Click here to turn on the
Slide Miniature window.

Click here to exit from
the Slide Master view.

FIGURE 8.3   The Slide Master ensures that all slides in a
presentation have a consistent look.

For most of PowerPoint's templates the Object Area sets up specifications for a bulleted list, including the type of bullet, as well as
the type styles, sizes, and indents for each item in the list.

In addition to the Title and Object Areas, the Slide Master can
contain information about background colors, borders, page numbers, company logos, clip art objects, and any other elements you
want to appear on every slide in the presentation.

The Slide Master is like any slide. In the following lessons, when
you learn how to add text, graphics, borders, and other objects to a
slide, keep in mind that you can add these objects on individual
slides or on the Slide Master. When you add the objects to the Slide
Master, the objects will appear on every slide in the presentation.

In this lesson, you learned how to give your presentation a consistent look with templates and AutoLayouts. You also learned how to
use the Slide Master to make global changes to your slides. In the
next lesson, you will learn how to insert, delete, and copy slides.

INSERTING, DELETING, AND COPYING SLIDES

In this lesson, you will learn how to insert new slides, delete slides, and copy slides in a presentation.

INSERTING A SLIDE

You can insert a slide into a presentation at any time and at any position in the presentation. To insert a slide, follow these steps:

1. Select the slide that appears just before the place where you want to insert the new slide. (You can select the slide in any view: Outline, Slides, Slide Sorter, or Notes Pages.)

2. Choose Insert, New Slide, click the New Slide button, or press Ctrl+M. In Outline view, PowerPoint inserts a blank slide, allowing you to type in a title and bulleted list. In all other views, the New Slide dialog box appears (see Figure 9.1).

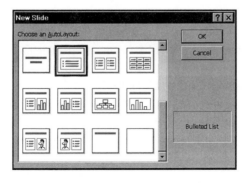

FIGURE 9.1 In the New Slide dialog box, you can choose a layout for the slide you're inserting.

3. In the Choose an AutoLayout list, click on a slide layout, or use the arrow keys to highlight it.

4. Click the OK button. PowerPoint inserts a slide that has the specified layout (see Figure 9.2).

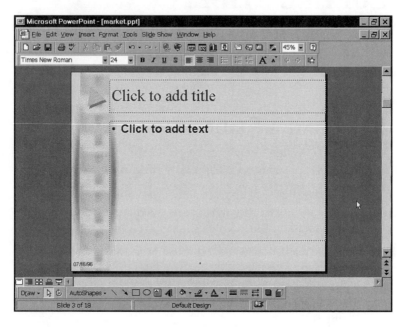

FIGURE 9.2 The new slide contains the blank structure you selected; you supply the content.

5. Follow the directions indicated on the slide layout to add text or other objects. In most cases, you click on an object to select it and then you type in your text.

Cloning a Slide To create an exact replica of a slide (in any view), select the slide you want to duplicate. Then select Insert, Duplicate Slide. The new slide is inserted after the original slide. You can move the slide anywhere you want, as you'll learn in Lesson 10.

New Feature!   The Insert, Duplicate Slide command is new for PowerPoint 97. In previous versions of PowerPoint, you could duplicate a slide only from Outline or Slide Sorter view, and you had to use the Edit, Duplicate command. This command is still available in those views in PowerPoint 97, so you can continue to use it if you are familiar with it.

ADDING SLIDES FROM ANOTHER PRESENTATION

If you want to insert some or all of the slides from another presentation into the current presentation, perform these steps:

1. Open the presentation into which you want to insert the slides.

2. Select the slide located before the position where you want to insert the slides.

3. Choose Insert, Slides from Files. The Slide Finder dialog box appears.

4. Click the Browse button to display the Insert Slides from Files dialog box.

5. Change the drive and/or folder if needed. (Refer to the section "Changing the Drive or Folder" in Lesson 6.)

6. Double-click on the name of the presentation that contains the slides you want to insert into the open presentation.

7. Click the Display button. The slides from the presentation appear in the Slide Finder window (see Figure 9.3).

Use this scroll bar to   Click here to insert   Click here to view the
move through the slides.   all the slides.   slides as a list with a
                                                     preview window.

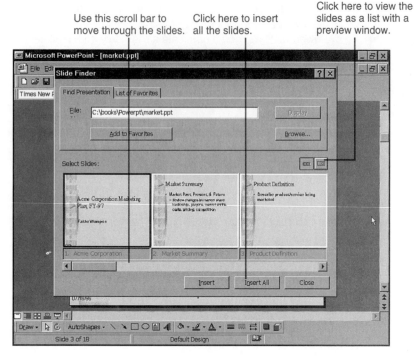

FIGURE 9.3   You can select any or all of the slides from the selected presentation to add to the open presentation.

 TIP   **View the Slides in a Different Way**   You can click this button if you prefer to see a list of the slide titles instead of three slides at a time. When you click the button, the display changes to a list of titles on the left and a preview window on the right that displays the selected slide.

8. Click the slides you want to insert and then click the Insert button. If you want to insert all the slides, click the Insert All button.

9. When you are finished inserting slides, click the Close button. The inserted slides appear right after the slide that you selected in step 2.

Make a Favorites List   If there is a presentation that you regularly use to insert slides from, you can add it to your Favorites List by clicking the Add to Favorites button in the Find Slides dialog box. Then the next time you want to insert slides from that presentation, just click the List of Favorites tab in the Find Slides dialog box and select the presentation from the list. You might, for example, have a presentation that contains some standard slides that you include in every presentation for a certain audience.

CREATING SLIDES FROM A DOCUMENT OUTLINE

If you have a word processing document with outline-style headings in it, PowerPoint can pull the headings from the document and use the headings to create slides with bulleted lists. To create slides from a document outline:

1. Choose Insert, Slides from Outline. The Insert Outline dialog box appears.

2. Use the Insert Outline dialog box to locate the document file you want to use. (Refer to "Changing the Drive or Folder" in Lesson 6 if you need help locating the file.)

3. Double-click on the name of the document file.

SELECTING SLIDES

In the following sections, you learn to delete, copy, and move slides. However, before you can do anything with a slide, you have to select the slide. To select slides, follow these directions:

- To select a single slide, click on it. (In Slide and Notes Pages views, the currently displayed slide is selected; you don't have to click on it.)

- To select two or more neighboring slides in Outline view, click on the first slide, and then hold down the Shift key while clicking on the last slide in the group.

- To select a rectangular block of neighboring slides in Slide Sorter view, click and drag a "box" around the slides you want to include. All slides that fall into the box you drag become selected (see Figure 9.4).

- To select two or more non-neighboring slides (in Slide Sorter view only), hold down the Ctrl and Shift key while clicking on each slide. You cannot select non-neighboring slides in Outline view.

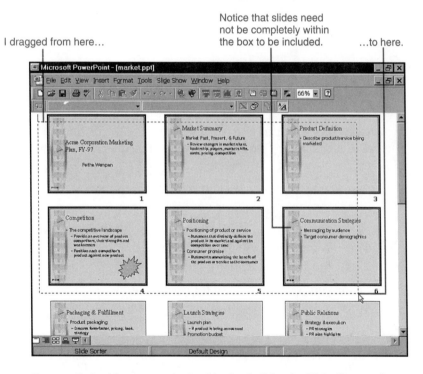

Figure 9.4   You can select a block of slides in Slide Sorter view by dragging a box around them.

Deleting Slides

You can delete a slide from any view. To delete a slide, perform the following steps:

1. Display the slide you want to delete (in Slide or Notes Pages view), or select the slide (in Outline or Slide Sorter view). You can delete multiple slides by displaying or selecting more than one slide.

2. Choose Edit, Delete Slide. The slide disappears.

 Quicker Deleting In Outline or Slide Sorter view, you can just select the slides you want to delete and press the Delete key on the keyboard.

 Oops! If you deleted a slide by mistake, you can get it back by selecting Edit, Undo, by pressing Ctrl+Z, or by clicking on the Undo button on the Standard toolbar.

CUTTING, COPYING, AND PASTING SLIDES

In Lesson 10, you will learn how to rearrange slides in Slide Sorter and Outline views. However, you also can use the cut, copy, and paste features to copy and move slides, either in the same presentation or into other presentations. To cut (or copy) a slide and paste it in a presentation, perform the following steps:

1. Change to Slide Sorter or Outline view.

2. Select the slide(s) you want to copy or cut.

3. Open the Edit menu, and select Cut or Copy to either move or copy the slide(s) to the Windows Clipboard.

 Windows Clipboard The Windows Clipboard is a temporary holding area for cut or copied items. You can cut or copy items to the Clipboard and then paste them on a slide, or cut or copy an entire slide or group of slides.

Quick Cut or Copy   To bypass the Edit menu, press
Ctrl+C to copy or Ctrl+X to cut, or click on the Cut or
Copy button on the Standard toolbar.

4. If you want to paste the slide(s) into a different presentation, open that presentation.

5. In Slide Sorter view, select the slide after which you want
to place the cut or copied slide(s). In Outline view, move
the insertion point to the end of the text in the slide after
which you want to insert the cut or copied slide(s).

 6. Choose Edit, Paste or press Ctrl+V. (You can also click on
the Paste button on the Standard toolbar.) PowerPoint
inserts the cut or copied slides.

 Drag and Drop   Although it's primarily used for moving
slides, drag-and-drop also can be used for copying them
in Slide Sorter view. You just drag a slide where you want
the copy to go, holding down the Ctrl key as you drag.
See Lesson 10 for details.

In this lesson, you learned how to insert, delete, cut, copy, and
paste slides. In the next lesson, you will learn how to rearrange
the slides in your presentation.

REARRANGING SLIDES IN A PRESENTATION

In this lesson, you will learn how to rearrange your slides.

There will be times when you need to change the sequence of slides in a presentation. PowerPoint has the capability to reorder slides in either Slide Sorter view or Outline view.

REARRANGING SLIDES IN SLIDE SORTER VIEW

Slide Sorter view shows miniature versions of the slides in your presentation. This enables you to view many of your slides at one time. To rearrange slides in Slide Sorter view, perform the following steps:

1. Switch to Slide Sorter view by selecting View, Slide Sorter, or clicking the Slide Sorter button on the status bar.

2. Move the mouse pointer over the slide you want to move.

3. Hold down the left mouse button, and drag the mouse pointer over the slide before or after which you want to insert the slide. As you drag the mouse pointer, a line appears (as shown in Figure 10.1), showing where you are moving the slide.

Slide Sorter button

This vertical line shows where
you are moving the slide.

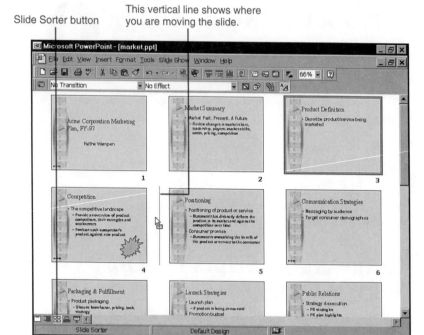

FIGURE 10.1 Switch to Slide Sorter view.

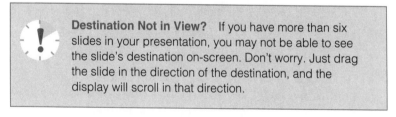

Destination Not in View? If you have more than six
slides in your presentation, you may not be able to see
the slide's destination on-screen. Don't worry. Just drag
the slide in the direction of the destination, and the
display will scroll in that direction.

4. Release the mouse button. PowerPoint places the slide in
its new position and shifts the surrounding slides to make
room for the new slide.

Copying a Slide You can copy a slide in Slide Sorter
view as easily as you can move a slide. Simply hold down
the Ctrl key while you drag the slide.

TIP **Dragging and Dropping Between Presentations** You can drag and drop slides to copy from one presentation to another. Open both presentations. (See Lesson 6 for instructions on how to open presentations.) Then choose Window, Arrange All. The two windows appear side-by-side. Change to Slide Sorter view in each window. You can now drag and drop slides from one window to the other.

REARRANGING SLIDES IN OUTLINE VIEW

In Outline view, you see the titles and text on each slide. This view gives you a clearer picture of the content and organization of your presentation than the other views, so you may prefer to rearrange your slides in Outline view. Here's how you do it:

1. Switch to Outline view by choosing View, Outline or clicking on the Outline button.

2. Click on the slide number or slide icon to the left of the slide you want to move. This action highlights the contents of the entire slide.

TIP **Moving the Contents of a Slide** If you just want to insert some of the information from a slide into your presentation, you don't have to move the entire slide. You can move only the slide's data—text and graphics—from one slide to another by selecting only what you want to move and dragging it to its new location.

3. Move the mouse pointer over the selected slide icon, hold down the mouse button, and drag the slide up or down in the outline, or click on the Move Up or Move Down buttons on the Outlining toolbar, as shown in Figure 10.2.

4. Release the mouse button when the slide is at the desired
new position. Be careful not to drop the slide in the
middle of another slide! If you do, just choose Edit, Undo
and try again.

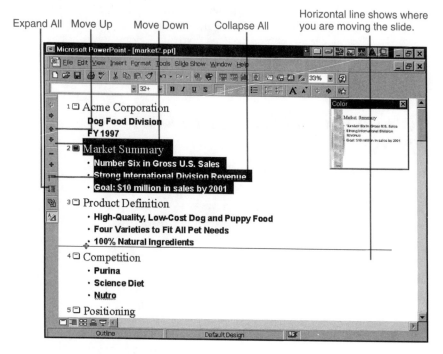

FIGURE 10.2 Drag the selected icon, or click on the Move Up or
Move Down button.

TIP   **Collapsing the Outline** You can collapse the outline to
show only the slide titles. This allows you to view more
slides at one time and rearrange the slides more easily.
To collapse the outline, click on the Collapse All button on
the Outlining toolbar (see Figure 10.2). To restore the
outline, click on the Expand All button.

HIDING SLIDES

Before you give a presentation, you should try to anticipate any questions that your audience may have and be prepared to answer those questions. You might even want to create slides to support your answers to these questions and then keep the slides hidden until you need them. To hide one or more slides, perform the following steps:

1. Display or select the slide(s) you want to hide. (You can hide slides in Slide, Outline, or Slide Sorter view.)

2. Choose Slide Show, Hide Slide from the menu. If you are in Slide Sorter view, the hidden slide's number appears in a box with a line through it.

3. To unhide the slide(s), display or select the hidden slide(s), and choose Slide Show, Hide Slide again.

 Right-Click Shortcut   You can right-click a slide and select Hide from the shortcut menu that appears to quickly hide a slide.

 Printing Hidden Slides?   In Lesson 7, you learned about the Print Hidden Slides check box in the Print dialog box. Select this check box when printing to print the hidden slides.

In this lesson, you learned how to rearrange the slides in a presentation in either the Slide Sorter or Outline view, and how to hide slides. In the next lesson, you will learn how to add text to a slide.

Lesson 11

ADDING TEXT TO A SLIDE

In this lesson, you will learn how to add text to a slide and change the text alignment and line spacing.

CREATING A TEXT BOX

As you have learned in previous lessons, you can put text on a slide by typing text in Outline view or filling in the blanks on an AutoLayout (see Lesson 9). However, these methods both provide fairly generic results. If you want to type additional text on a slide, you must first create a text box.

 Text Box A text box acts as a receptacle for the text. Text boxes often contain bulleted lists, notes, and labels (used to point to important parts of illustrations).

To create a text box, perform the following steps:

1. Switch to Slide view or Slide Sorter view. (Refer to Lesson 5 for help with views.) Slide view may give you a clearer view of your work area than Slide Sorter view.

2. If you want the text box to appear on a new slide, insert a slide into the presentation. (Choose Insert, Slide; see Lesson 9 for details.)

 3. Click on the Text Box button on the Drawing toolbar.

4. Move the mouse pointer to where you want the upper-left corner of the box to appear.

5. Hold down the left mouse button and drag the mouse pointer to the right until the box is the desired width. (It doesn't matter how far you drag down vertically; the box created will always be the same height—one line.)

6. Release the mouse button. A one-line text box appears (see Figure 11.1).

Text you type will appear here.

Selection handles

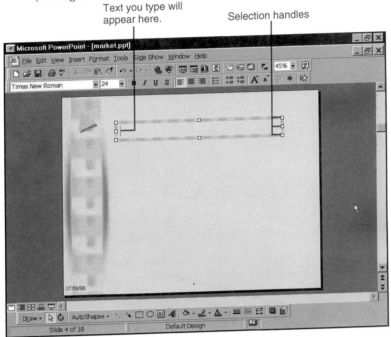

FIGURE 11.1   You can enter text in the text box.

7. Type the text that you want to appear in the text box. When you reach the right side of the box, PowerPoint wraps the text to the next line and makes the box one line deeper. To start a new paragraph, press Enter.

8. When you are done, click anywhere outside the text box to see how the text will appear on the finished slide.

Framing a Text Box   The border that appears around a text box when you create or select it does not appear on the printed slide. To add a border that does print, see Lesson 16.

SELECTING, DELETING, AND MOVING A TEXT BOX

If you go back and click anywhere inside the text box, a selection box appears around it. If you click on the selection box border, handles appear around the text box, as shown in Figure 11.1. You can drag the box's border to move the box, or drag a handle to resize it. PowerPoint wraps the text automatically as needed to fit inside the box.

To delete a text box, select it (so handles appear around it), and then press the Delete key.

EDITING TEXT IN A TEXT BOX

To edit text in a text box, first click anywhere inside the text box to select it; then, perform any of the following steps:

- To select text, drag the I-beam pointer over the text you want to select. (To select a single word, double-click on it. To select an entire paragraph, triple-click.)

Auto Word Select When you drag over text, PowerPoint selects whole words. If you want to select individual characters, select Tools, Options, click the Edit tab, and deselect the Automatic Word Selection check box.

- To delete text, select the text and press the Delete key. You can also use the Delete or Backspace keys to delete single characters to the right or left of the insertion point, respectively.

- To insert text, click the I-beam pointer where you want to insert the text and type the text.

- To replace text, select the text you want to replace and type the new text. When you start typing, PowerPoint deletes the selected text.

- To copy and paste text, select the text you want to copy and choose Edit, Copy, click the Copy button on the Standard toolbar, or press Ctrl+C. Move the insertion point to where you want the text pasted (it can be in a different text box) and choose Edit, Paste, click the Paste button, or press Ctrl+V.

- To cut and paste (move) text, select the text you want to cut and choose Edit, Cut, click the Cut button on the Standard toolbar, or press Ctrl+X. Move the insertion point to where you want the text pasted (it can be in a different text box), and choose Edit, Paste, click the Paste button, or press Ctrl+V.

Changing the Text Alignment and Line Spacing

When you first type text, PowerPoint automatically sets it against the left edge of the text box. To change the paragraph alignment, perform the following steps:

1. Click anywhere inside the paragraph you want to realign.

2. Select Format, Alignment. The Alignment submenu appears.

3. Select Left, Center, Right, or Justify, to align the paragraph as desired. (See Figure 11.2 for examples.)

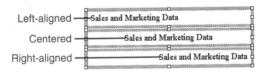

Figure 11.2   You can align each paragraph in a text box.

Some Alignment Shortcuts   To quickly set left alignment, press Ctrl+L or click the Left Alignment button on the Formatting toolbar. To quickly apply right alignment, press Ctrl+R or click the Right Alignment button. To quickly apply centered alignment, press Ctrl+C or click the Center Alignment button.

The default setting for line spacing is single-space. To change the line spacing in a paragraph, perform these steps:

1. Click inside the paragraph you want to change, or select all the paragraphs you want to change.

2. Select Format, Line Spacing. The Line Spacing dialog box appears, as shown in Figure 11.3.

FIGURE 11.3   The Line Spacing dialog box.

3. Click on the arrow buttons to the right of any of the following text boxes to change the line spacing:

   Line Spacing   This setting controls the space between the lines in a paragraph.

   Before Paragraph   This setting controls the space between this paragraph and the paragraph that comes before it.

   After Paragraph   This setting controls the space between this paragraph and the paragraph that comes after it.

Lines or Points? The drop-down list box that appears to the right of each setting allows you to set the line spacing in lines or points. A line is the current line height (based on text size). A point is a unit commonly used to measure text. A point is approximately 1/72 of an inch.

4. Click OK.

ADDING A WORDART OBJECT

PowerPoint comes with an auxiliary program called WordArt that can help you create graphic text effects. To insert a WordArt object into a slide, perform the following steps:

1. Display the slide on which you want to place the WordArt object in Slide view.

2. Click the WordArt button on the Drawing toolbar (at the bottom of the screen). The WordArt Gallery dialog box appears, showing many samples of WordArt types.

3. Click on the sample that best represents the WordArt type you want, and then click OK. The Edit WordArt Text dialog box appears (see Figure 11.4).

4. Choose a font and size from the respective drop-down lists.

5. Type the text you want to use in the Text box (see Figure 11.4).

FIGURE 11.4 Enter the text, size, and font to be used into the Edit WordArt Text dialog box.

6. Click OK. PowerPoint creates the WordArt text on your slide, as shown in Figure 11.5.

After you have created some WordArt, you have access to the WordArt toolbar, shown in Figure 11.5. You can use it to modify your WordArt. Table 11.1 summarizes the buttons on that toolbar.

WordArt toolbar   WordArt text

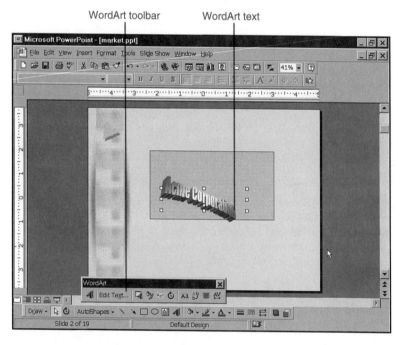

FIGURE 11.5 Here is some finished WordArt on a slide. Notice the WordArt toolbar below it.

TABLE 11.1   BUTTONS ON THE WORDART TOOLBAR

BUTTON	PURPOSE
◀	Creates a new WordArt object
Edit Text...	Edits the text, size, and font of the selected WordArt object

BUTTON	PURPOSE
	Changes the type of the current WordArt object
	Changes the Line and Fill color
	Changes the WordArt shape
	Rotates the WordArt object
	Makes all the letters the same height
	Changes between vertical and horizontal text orientation
	Changes the text alignment
	Changes the spacing between letters

To edit the WordArt object, double-click on it to display the WordArt toolbar and text entry box. Enter your changes; then, click outside the WordArt object. You can move the object by dragging its border, or resize it by dragging a handle.

In this lesson, you learned how to add text to a slide, change the text alignment and spacing, and add WordArt objects. In the next lesson, you will learn how to use tables, tabs, and indents to create columns and lists.

12 LESSON CREATING COLUMNS AND LISTS

In this lesson, you will learn how to use tabs to create columns of text and use indents to create bulleted lists, numbered lists, and other types of lists.

USING TABS TO CREATE COLUMNS

A presentation often uses tabbed columns to display information. For example, you may use tabs to create a three-column list like the one shown in Figure 12.1.

In addition to hardware products, we carry a varied line of software:

Business	Home	Education
WordPerfect	Quicken	Reader Rabbit 2
Microsoft Word	The New Print Shop	Oregon Trail
PowerPoint	Microsoft Works	BodyWorks
Excel	TurboTax	Where in the World is Carmen Sandiego?

FIGURE 12.1 You can use tabs to create a multicolumn list.

In PowerPoint, you create multiple columns using tab stops. To set the tabs for a multicolumn list, perform the following steps:

1. Open the presentation and view the slide you want to work with in Slide View.

2. Create a text box for the text. (For instructions on how to create a text box, see Lesson 11.)

3. Click anywhere inside the text box for which you want to set the tabs.

4. If you already typed text inside the text box, select the text.

5. Select View, Ruler to display the ruler, if it does not already appear.

6. Click on the tab icon in the upper-left corner of the presentation window until it represents the type of tab you want to set.

7. Click on each place in the ruler where you want to set the selected type of tab stop, as shown in Figure 12.2.

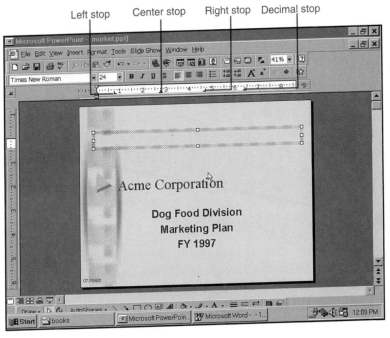

FIGURE 12.2 The ruler lets you enter and change tab stop settings.

L	Aligns the left end of the line against the tab stop.
⊥	Centers the text on the tab stop.
⌐	Aligns the right end of the line against the tab stop.

Aligns the tab stop on a period. This is called a decimal tab and is useful for aligning a column of numbers that uses decimal points.

8. Repeat steps 4 and 5 if you want to set different types of tab stops at different positions.

9. To change the position of an existing tab stop setting, drag it on the ruler to the desired position. To delete an existing tab stop setting, drag it off the ruler.

10. (Optional) To turn off the ruler, select View, Ruler.

 Don't Forget the Slide Master   Throughout this lesson, keep in mind that you can enter your changes on the Slide Master or on individual slides. If you change the Slide Master, the change affects all slides in the presentation. For details on displaying the Slide Master, see Lesson 8.

MAKING A BULLETED LIST

When you enter new slides in Outline view, the default layout is a simple bulleted list. If you've done this (see Lesson 9), you've already created a bulleted list. However, you can also create one in a text box that you add to a slide yourself, without relying on an AutoLayout. Just follow these steps to change some regular text in a text box to a bulleted list:

1. Click inside the paragraph you want to transform into a bulleted list, or select one or more paragraphs.

2. Select Format, Bullet. The Bullet dialog box appears.

  Quick Bullets   To bypass the Format menu and Bullet dialog box, simply click the Bullet button on the Formatting toolbar to insert a bullet, or right-click and select Bullet from the shortcut menu. You can click on the Bullet button again to remove the bullet.

3. Select the Use a Bullet check box to enable bullet use.

4. Click OK. PowerPoint transforms the selected text into a bulleted list. (If you press Enter at the end of a bulleted paragraph, the next paragraph starts with a bullet.)

Moving a Bulleted Item You can move an item in a bulleted list by clicking on the item's bullet and then **TIP** dragging the bullet up or down in the list.

CHANGING THE BULLET CHARACTER

By default, whenever you click on the Bullet button on the Formatting toolbar to insert a bullet, PowerPoint inserts a large dot for the bullet. However, you can change the appearance of the bullet at any time by following these steps:

1. Select the paragraph(s) in which you want to change the bullet character.

2. Select Format, Bullet. The Bullet dialog box appears (see Figure 12.3).

When you click on a character, PowerPoint shows it enlarged.

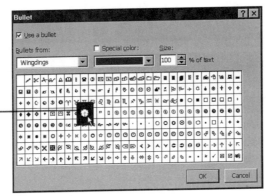

FIGURE 12.3 The Bullet dialog box lets you choose an alternate bullet character.

3. Pull down the Bullets From list, and select the character set from which you want to choose a bullet. The dialog box displays the characters in the selected set.

Which Character Set? Each character set is nothing more than a font that's installed on your computer. Some fonts are better suited for bullets than others—open several and examine the characters each one contains. Wingdings is a good choice.

4. Click on the character you want to use for the bullet. When you click on a character, PowerPoint shows it enlarged so you can see it clearly, as shown in Figure 12.3.

5. To set the size of the bullet, use the up and down arrows to the right of the Size text box. Notice that the size of the bullet is not a fixed value—it is relative to the text around it.

6. To select a color for the bullet, pull down the Special Color drop-down list and select the desired color.

7. Click OK. PowerPoint changes the bullet character for all selected paragraphs.

Using Indents to Create Lists

Indents allow you to move one or more lines of a paragraph in from the left margin. PowerPoint uses indents to create the bulleted lists you encountered in previous lessons. You can use indents in any text object to create a similar list or your own custom list. To indent text, perform the following steps:

1. Select the text box that contains the text you want to indent.

2. If you already typed text, select the text you want to indent.

3. If the ruler is not visible, select View, Ruler.

4. Drag one of the following indent markers to set the indents for the paragraph. (These indent markers appear on the ruler, as shown in Figure 12.4.)

 Drag the top marker to indent the first line.

 Drag the bottom marker to indent all subsequent lines.

 Drag the box below the bottom marker to indent all the text.

5. (Optional) To turn the ruler off, select View, Ruler.

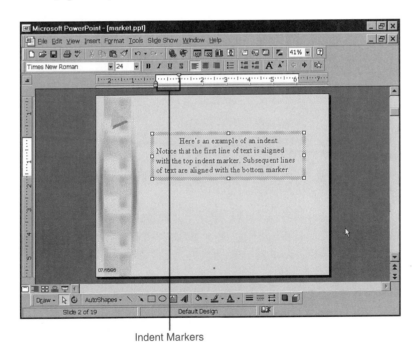

Indent Markers

FIGURE 12.4 Drag the indent markers to indent your text.

You can create up to five levels of indents within a single text box. To add an indent level, click on the Demote button on the Formatting toolbar, or press Tab when the insertion point is at the beginning of the paragraph. A new set of indent markers appears on the ruler, showing the next level of indents. You can change these new indent settings as explained previously.

Once you have set your indents, you can create a numbered or bulleted list by performing the following steps:

1. Type a number and a period, or type the character you want to use for the bullet.

2. Press the Tab key to move to the second indent mark.

3. Type the text you want to use for this item. As you type, PowerPoint wraps the text to the second indent mark.

4. Repeat steps 1 through 3 for each additional item you add to the list.

In this lesson, you learned how to create columns with tabs, create lists with indents, and change the bullet character for bulleted lists. In the next lesson, you will learn how to change the style, size, and color of text.

CHANGING THE LOOK OF YOUR TEXT

In this lesson, you will learn how to change the appearance of text by changing its font, style, size, and color.

ENHANCING YOUR TEXT WITH THE FONT DIALOG BOX

You can enhance your text by using the Font dialog box or by using various tools on the Formatting toolbar. Use the Font dialog box if you want to add several enhancements to your text at one time. Use the Formatting toolbar to add one enhancement at a time.

Fonts, Styles, and Effects In PowerPoint, a *font* is a family of text that has the same design or typeface (for example, Arial or Courier). A *style* is a standard enhancement, such as bold or italic. An *effect* is a special enhancement, such as shadow or underline.

You can change the font of existing text or of text you are about to type by performing the following steps:

1. To change the font of existing text, select text by dragging the I-beam pointer over the text.

2. Choose Format, Font. The Font dialog box appears, as shown in Figure 13.1.

Right-Click Quick You can right-click on the text and select Font from the shortcut menu instead of performing steps 1 and 2.

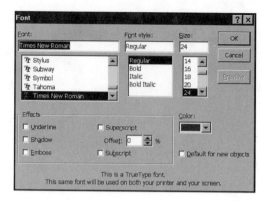

Figure 13.1   You can select a font in the Font dialog box.

3. From the Font list, select the font you want to use.

TrueType Fonts   The TT next to a font name identifies the font as a TrueType font. TrueType fonts are *scalable*, which means you can set them at any point size. When you save a presentation, you can choose to embed TrueType fonts so you can display or print the font on any computer whether or not it has that font installed.

4. From the Font Style list, select any style you want to apply to the text. (To remove styles from text, select Regular.)

5. From the Size list, select any size in the list, or type a size directly into the box. (With TrueType fonts, you can type any point size, even sizes that do not appear on the list.)

6. In the Effects group, select any special effects you want to add to the text, such as Underline, Shadow, or Emboss. You can also choose Superscript or Subscript, though these are less common.

7. To change the color of your text, click on the arrow button to the right of the Color list, and click on the desired color. (For more colors, click on the More Colors option at the bottom of the list and use the dialog box that appears to select a color.)

Changing the Background Color   Each presentation has its own color scheme, which includes background and text colors. You'll learn about creating and changing color schemes in Lesson 17.

8. Click OK to apply the new look to your text. (If you selected text before styling it, the text appears in the new style. If you did not select text, any text you type appears in the new style.)

Title and Object Area Text   If you change a font on an individual slide, the font change applies only to that slide. To change the font for all the slides in the presentation, you need to change the font on the Slide Master. To change the Slide Master, select View, Master, Slide Master. Select a text area and perform the steps shown here to change the look of the text on all slides.

STYLING TEXT WITH THE FORMATTING TOOLBAR

As shown in Figure 13.2, the Formatting toolbar contains several tools for changing the font, size, style, and color of text.

To use the tools, follow these steps:

1. To change the look of existing text, select the text.

2. To change fonts, open the Font drop-down list (see Figure 13.2) and click on the desired font.

3. To change font size, open the Font Size drop-down list (shown in Figure 13.2) and click on the desired size, or type a size directly into the box.

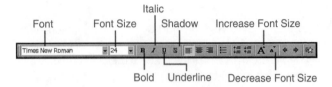

FIGURE 13.2   The Formatting toolbar contains several tools for styling text.

Incrementing the Type Size   To increase or decrease the text size to the next size up or down, click on the Increase Font Size or Decrease Font Size buttons on the Formatting toolbar.

4. To add a style or effect to the text (bold, italic, underline, and/or shadow), click on the appropriate button(s):

B   Bold

I   Italic

U   Underline

S   Shadow

CHANGING FONT COLOR WITH THE DRAWING TOOLBAR

New Location for Font Color Button   In earlier versions of PowerPoint, the Font Color button was on the Formatting toolbar rather than the Drawing toolbar.

The Font Color button on the Drawing toolbar (at the bottom of the screen) enables you to change the color of the selected text.

Just do the following:

1. Select the text for which you want to change the color.

2. Click the down-pointing arrow next to the Font Color button on the Drawing toolbar. A menu of options appears (see Figure 13.3).

3. Do one of the following:

   • Click on one of the colored blocks to change the font to one of the pre-chosen colors for the presentation design you're using.

   • Click the More Font Colors button to display a Colors dialog box, and then click on a color in that box and click OK.

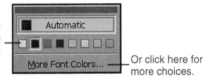

Click on one of these pre-selected colors to stay within the presentation design's color scheme.

Automatic

More Font Colors...

Or click here for more choices.

FIGURE 13.3 When you click the arrow next to the Font Colors button, this menu of options appears.

COPYING TEXT FORMATS

If your presentation contains text with a format you want to use, you can pick up the format from the existing text and apply it to other text. To copy text formats, perform the following steps:

1. Highlight the text with the format you want to use.

2. Click the Format Painter button on the toolbar. PowerPoint copies the format.

3. Drag the mouse pointer across the text to which you want to apply the format.

In this lesson, you learned how to change the appearance of text by changing its font, size, style, and color. You also learned how to copy text formats. In the next lesson, you will learn how to draw objects on a slide.

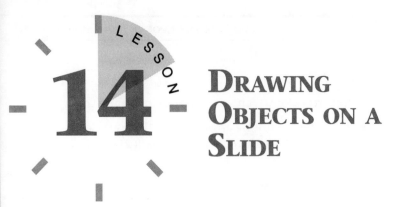

14 DRAWING OBJECTS ON A SLIDE

In this lesson, you will learn how to use PowerPoint's drawing tools to draw graphic objects on a slide.

POWERPOINT'S DRAWING TOOLS

Although PowerPoint is not a drawing program per se, you can do some simple drawing with it. For example, you may want to draw a simple logo, or accent your slide with horizontal or vertical lines.

To this end, PowerPoint comes with several drawing tools to help you create lines and shapes. The Drawing toolbar displays these tools along the bottom of the presentation window in Slide and Notes Pages views.

There are two types of tools on the Drawing toolbar: tools for drawing lines and shapes and tools for manipulating the graphic objects. Here's a look at the drawing ones:

Tool	Purpose
	Draws a straight line
	Draws a straight line with an arrow on the end
	Draws a rectangle
	Draws an ellipse (oval)

DRAWING A LINE OR SHAPE

The general procedure for drawing an object is the same, no matter which object you draw:

1. Click on the button on the Drawing toolbar for the line or shape you want to draw. For example, to draw a rectangle, click on the Rectangle button.

2. Move the mouse pointer to where you want one end of the line or one corner of the object to be anchored.

3. Hold down the mouse button, and drag to where you want the opposite end of the line or corner of the object to appear. Figure 14.1 shows the procedure for drawing a rectangle.

4. Release the mouse button. The finished line or shape appears.

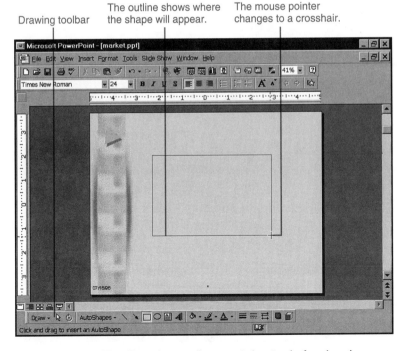

FIGURE 14.1 The Drawing toolbar contains tools for drawing lines and basic shapes.

> **Squares and Circles**   You can draw a perfect square
> or circle by holding down the Shift key as you use the
> Rectangle or Ellipse tool, respectively.

WORKING WITH AUTOSHAPES

Drawing a complex shape with the rudimentary tools available to
you can be frustrating. That's why PowerPoint comes with several
predrawn objects, called AutoShapes, that you can use. To draw
one of these objects, perform the following steps:

`AutoShapes ▾` **1.** Click on the AutoShapes tool on the Drawing toolbar. A
menu of shape types appears.

2. Click on the type of shape you want. For example, if you
want an arrow, choose Block Arrows. The AutoShapes
palette appears for that type of shape, as shown in
Figure 14.2.

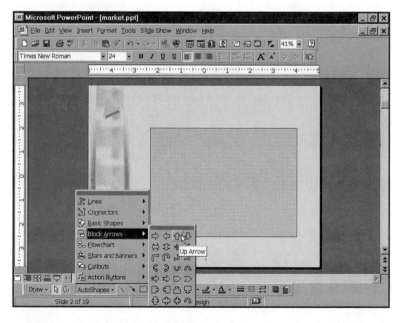

FIGURE 14.2   Select the shape you want from the AutoShapes
palette.

3. Click on the shape you want to draw.

4. Move the mouse pointer to where you want a corner or the center of the shape to be.

5. (Optional) While drawing the object, hold down one or both of the following keys: Ctrl to draw the shape out from a center point, or Shift to draw a shape that retains the dimensions shown on the AutoShapes palette.

6. Hold down the mouse button and drag the mouse to draw the object.

7. Release the mouse button. The shape appears, as shown in Figure 14.3.

TIP **Changing an Existing Shape** You can change an existing shape into a different shape. Select the shape you want to change, click the Draw button on the Drawing toolbar, select Change AutoShape, and click on the shape you want to use.

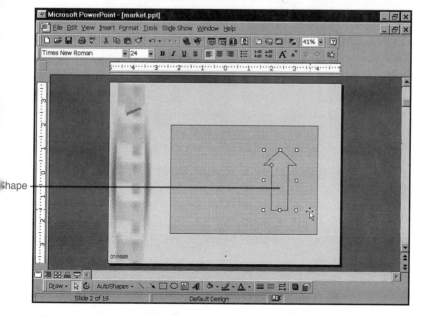

FIGURE 14.3 You can draw an AutoShape like this arrow as easily as any simple rectangle.

ADDING TEXT TO AN OBJECT

You can add text to an object you draw. Unlike overlaying a shape with a text box, text typed into a shape stays with the shape when you move it. To insert text into your drawing, follow these steps:

1. Click on the object in which you want the text to appear.

2. Type the text. As you type, the text appears in a single line across the object.

3. (Optional) Select Format, AutoShape. The Format AutoShape dialog box appears.

4. Click the Text Box tab to display the options shown in Figure 14.4.

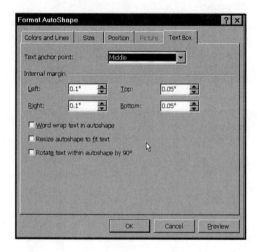

FIGURE 14.4   Use the Text Box tab to position your text inside the object.

5. Open the Text Anchor Point drop-down list and choose a position for the text in relation to the shape. (Middle is the default.)

6. Set margins for all four sides of the shape (Left, Right, Top, and Bottom), establishing how much white space will be left between the edges of the shape and the text.

7. (Optional) Select any of the following check boxes:

- **Word Wrap Text in Autoshape**   Wraps text to another line if the text is wider than the shape.

- **Resize Authoshape to Fit Text**   Makes the shape larger or smaller so the text fits exactly within the margins you specify in step 5.

- **Rotate Text Within Autoshape by 90°**   Rotates the text to run the other way (usually vertically) to help it fit better in the shape.

 TIP   **Viewing the Effects of Your Changes**   You can drag the title bar of the dialog box to move the dialog box away from the object. Then you can view the effects of your changes by clicking the Preview button before you click OK to save your changes.

8. Click OK to save your changes.

You can change the style and alignment of the text in an object in the same way you can change style and alignment in any text box. Refer to Lessons 11, 12, and 13 for details.

Tips for Working with Objects

Here are some quick tips that can save you some time and reduce frustration as you begin working with objects. You'll learn more about manipulating objects in Lessons 15 and 16.

- If you're going to use the same tool to draw several objects in a row, double-click on the tool. The tool stays selected and you don't have to re-click it after you draw each shape.

- To draw an object out from the center rather than from a corner, hold down the Ctrl key while dragging.

- To select an object, click on it.

- To delete an object, select it and press Delete.

- To move an object, select it and drag one of its lines.

- To resize or reshape an object, select it and drag one of its handles.

- To copy an object, hold down the Ctrl key while dragging it.

In this lesson, you learned how to use PowerPoint's drawing tools to add drawings to your slides. In the next lesson, you will learn how to add clip art, pictures, sounds, and video clips to your slides.

ADDING PICTURES, SOUNDS, AND VIDEO CLIPS

15

In this lesson, you will learn how to add PowerPoint clip art, pictures from other graphics programs, sounds, and video clips to a slide.

INTRODUCING THE CLIP GALLERY

Microsoft has taken a bold new step in the Office 97 products (of which PowerPoint is one) in handling multiple media such as sounds, videos, and artwork. It's called the Clip Gallery (see Figure 15.1).

Each type of object has its own tab

Previews of objects in the chosen category

Internet icon

List of categories

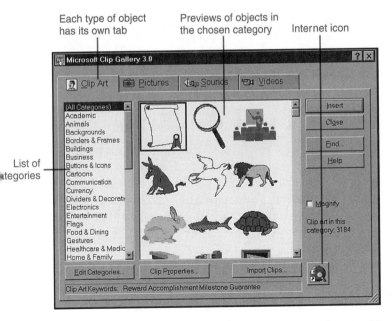

FIGURE 15.1 The Clip Gallery manages pictures, clip art, videos, and sounds, all in one convenient place.

Clip Art Clip art is a collection of previously created images or pictures that you can place on a slide.

You can open the Clip Gallery in any of these ways:

- Click on the Clip Art button on the Standard toolbar.
- Select Insert, Picture, Clip Art.
- Select Insert, Movies and Sounds, Sound from Gallery.
- Select Insert, Movies and Sounds, Movie from Gallery.

All of these methods open the Clip Gallery, but a different tab appears on top depending on which method you used. For example, if you use Insert, Picture, Clip Art, the Clip Art tab appears on top, as shown in Figure 15.1.

 PowerPoint on the Web Click the Internet icon in the corner of the Clip Gallery 3.0 dialog box (shown in Figure 15.1) to connect to Microsoft's Web site and download additional clip art.

INSERTING A CLIP ON A SLIDE

Using the Clip Gallery, you can place any of the four types of objects on a slide: clip art, picture, sound, or movie. In the case of the latter two, you then click on the object to activate it as needed during the presentation. For example, you click on the sound's icon to make it play. You also can set up sounds and movies to play automatically when a slide displays, as you'll learn later in this lesson.

To insert a clip onto a slide, follow these steps:

1. Open the Clip Gallery, as described in the previous section.

2. Click on the tab for the type of clip you want to insert.

3. Click on the category that represents the type of clip you want.

4. Click on the clip you want to use.

5. Click the Insert button.

The Clip I Want Isn't on the List!   If you don't see the clip you're looking for, click the Import Clips button and use the dialog box that appears to locate the clip and import it into the Clip Gallery. From then on, that image will be available on the appropriate Clip Gallery tab for its file type.

File Size on the Web   Artwork, movies, and sounds can really add a lot to a PowerPoint presentation on the Web, but they also add to the size of the file, and consequently, to the time it will take a reader to download it. For this reason, try to be judicious in your use of media on presentations designed for Web use.

INSERTING A CLIP FROM A FILE

If you have a clip stored on disk, such as a bitmap image, sound file, or movie file, you can quickly place it on a slide without using with the Clip Gallery. Just follow these steps.

To place a graphics image from disk on a slide:

1. Select the slide on which the image should be placed.

2. Select Insert, Picture, Picture From File. The Insert Picture dialog box appears (see Figure 15.2).

Preview
button

FIGURE 15.2 Use the Insert Picture dialog box to place any graphics image on a slide.

3. Select the picture you want to use. You can see a preview of the pictures in the Preview pane to the left of the file list. If the preview does not appear, click the Preview button (shown in Figure 15.2) to turn the preview feature on.

4. Click Insert to place the image on the slide.

If the picture is too big or too small, you can drag the selection handles (the small squares) around the edge of the image to resize it. (Hold down Shift to proportionally resize.) Refer to Lesson 16 for more details about resizing and cropping.

TIP

Movies and Sounds from Files You also can insert movies and sounds from files. Just select Insert, Movies and Sounds, and then either Movie from File or Sound from File.

CHOOSING WHEN MOVIES AND SOUNDS SHOULD PLAY

Slides are static, for the most part. They appear and then they sit there. Movies and sounds, on the other hand, are dynamic—they play at certain times.

The default when you place a movie or sound on a slide is that the object does not activate until you click on it. A slide may contain, for example, a recorded narration that explains a particular graph on the slide, but the narration will not play until the person giving the presentation clicks on the sound icon to activate it.

However, you may want some sounds or movies to play automatically at certain times in the presentation. You control this with the following procedure:

1. Click on the object (the sound icon or movie image) on the slide.

2. Select Slide Show, Custom Animation. The Custom Animation dialog box appears (see Figure 15.3).

3. Choose the Timing tab.

4. Click the Animate button to indicate that you want the sound or movie to play on the slide.

5. Click the Automatically button to indicate you want it to play without user intervention.

6. In the text box next to the Automatically control, enter the number of seconds that PowerPoint should pause after the previous event before playing the object.

 Previous Event?   If this is the only media clip on this slide, the previous event is the slide itself being displayed. If there is more than one media clip on the slide, you can control which order they activate in by switching around their order in the Animation order list in the Custom Animation dialog box (see Figure 15.3).

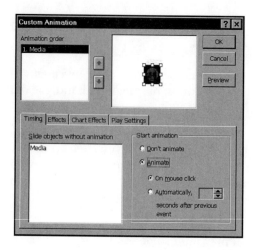

FIGURE 15.3   Use this dialog box to set when and how a sound or movie plays.

7. Click OK.

 8. Switch to Slide Show view to test the slide, making sure you have set up the sound or animation to play when you want it to.

 Continuous Play   You can set a sound or animation to loop continuously by clicking the Play Settings tab, then the More Options button. Select both the Loop Until Stopped and Rewind Movie When Done Playing check boxes.

In this lesson, you learned how to add clip art images, pictures, sounds, and movies to your slides, and how to control when a movie or sound plays. In the next lesson, you will learn how to reposition and resize objects on a slide.

Positioning and Sizing Objects

In this lesson, you will learn how to select, copy, move, rotate, and resize objects on a slide.

As you may have already discovered, objects are the building blocks you use to create slides in PowerPoint. Objects are the shapes you draw, the graphs you create, the pictures you import, and the text you type. In this and the next lesson, you will learn how to manipulate objects on your slides to create impressive presentations.

Selecting Objects

Before you can copy, move, rotate, or resize an object, you must first select the object. Change to Slide view, and perform one of the following steps to choose one or more objects:

- To select a single object, click on it. (If you click on text, a frame appears around the text. Click on the frame to select the text object.)

- To select more than one object, hold down the Shift key while clicking on each object. Handles appear around the selected objects, as shown in Figure 16.1.

- To deselect selected objects, click anywhere outside the selected objects.

Selection tool   Selection handles

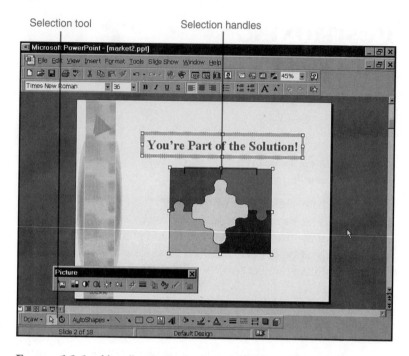

FIGURE 16.1   Handles indicate that objects are selected.

> **Using the Selection Tool**   The Selection tool on the
> **TIP**   Drawing toolbar (the button with the mouse pointer on it),
> enables you to quickly select a group of objects. Click on
> the Selection tool and use the mouse pointer to drag a
> selection box around the objects you want to select.
> When you release the mouse button, PowerPoint selects
> the objects inside the box.

WORKING WITH LAYERS OF OBJECTS

As you place objects on-screen, they may start to overlap, making
it difficult or impossible to select the objects in the lower layers.
To move objects in layers, perform the following steps:

1. Click on the object you want to move up or down in the
   stack.

2. Click the Draw button on the Drawing toolbar to open the Draw menu, and select Order, as shown in Figure 16.2.

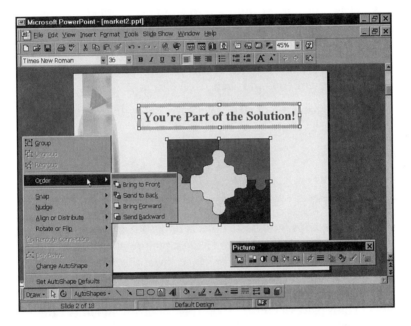

FIGURE 16.2 Use the Draw menu on the Drawing toolbar to change the layer on which a graphic appears on your slide.

3. Select one of the following options:

- **Bring to Front** brings the object to the top of the stack.

- **Send to Back** sends the object to the bottom of the stack.

- **Bring Forward** brings the object up one layer.

- **Send Backward** sends the object back one layer.

GROUPING AND UNGROUPING OBJECTS

Each object you draw acts as an individual object. However, sometimes you want two or more objects to act as a group. For example, you may want to make the lines of several objects the same thickness, or group several objects together. If you want to treat two or more objects as a group, perform the following steps:

1. Select the objects you want to group. Remember, to select more than one object, hold down the Shift key as you click on each one.

2. Click the Draw button on the Drawing toolbar to open the Draw menu, and then select Group.

3. To ungroup the objects, select any object in the group, and select Draw, Ungroup.

CUTTING, COPYING, AND PASTING OBJECTS

You can cut, copy, and paste objects on a slide to rearrange the objects or to use the objects to create a picture. When you cut an object, PowerPoint removes the object from the slide and places it in a temporary holding area called the Windows Clipboard. When you copy an object, the original object remains on the slide, and PowerPoint places a copy of it on the Clipboard. In either case, you can then paste the object from the Clipboard onto the current slide or another slide. To cut or copy an object, perform the following steps:

1. Select the object(s) you want to cut, copy, or move.

 2. Right-click on the selection and choose Cut or Copy from the shortcut menu. Or, select Edit, Cut or Edit, Copy, or click the Cut or Copy buttons on the Standard toolbar.

3. Display the slide on which you want to place the cut or copied object(s). (You can also open a different Windows program, to paste it into, if you prefer.)

4. Select Edit, Paste, or click on the Paste button on the Standard toolbar. PowerPoint pastes the object(s) on the slide.

Keyboard Shortcuts   You can press Ctrl+X to cut, Ctrl+C to copy, and Ctrl+V to paste instead of using the toolbar buttons or the menu.

5. Move the mouse pointer over any of the pasted objects, hold down the mouse button, and drag the objects to where you want them.

6. Release the mouse button.

Deleting an Object   To remove an object without placing it on the Clipboard, select the object and then press the Delete key, or select Edit, Clear.

Dragging and Dropping Objects   The quickest way to copy or move objects is to drag and drop them. Select the objects you want to move, position the mouse pointer over any of the selected objects, hold down the mouse button, and drag the objects where you want them. To copy the objects, hold down the Ctrl key while dragging.

ROTATING AN OBJECT

The Rotate tools enable you to revolve an object around a center point.

To rotate an object to your own specifications, using Free Rotate, do the following:

1. Click on the object you want to rotate.

2. Click the Free Rotate tool on the Drawing toolbar. The selection handles on the centering line change to circles.

3. Hold down the mouse button and drag the circular handle until the object is in the position you want. (See Figure 16.3.)

4. Release the mouse button.

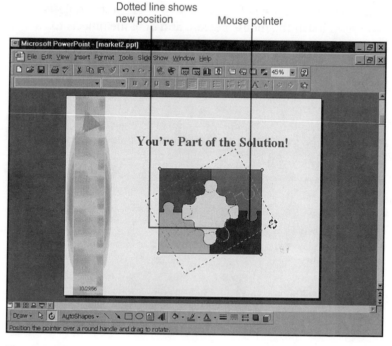

Figure 16.3   You can drag the circular selection handle to rotate the object.

TIP

Other Rotate Options   The Draw menu (on the Drawing toolbar; refer to Figure 16.2) contains a Rotate or Flip submenu that provides additional options for rotating objects. You can flip an object 90 degrees left or right, or flip the object over on the centering line to create a mirrored image of it.

RESIZING OBJECTS

There may be times when an object you create or import is not the right size for your slide presentation. You can resize the object by performing these steps:

1. Select the object to resize. Selection handles appear.

2. Drag one of the handles (the squares that surround the object) until the object is the desired size:

   - Drag a corner handle to change both the height and width of an object. PowerPoint retains the object's relative dimensions.

   - Drag a side, top, or bottom handle to change the height or width alone.

   - Hold down the Ctrl key while dragging to resize from the center of the picture.

3. Release the mouse button, and PowerPoint resizes the object (see Figure 16.4).

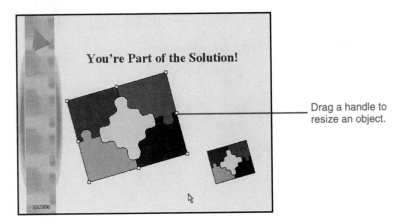

Drag a handle to resize an object.

FIGURE 16.4   Before and after resizing an object.

CROPPING A PICTURE

Besides resizing a picture, you can crop it. That is, you can trim a side or corner of the picture to remove an element from the picture or cut off some white space. To crop a picture, perform the following steps:

1. Click on the picture you want to crop.

2. If the Picture toolbar isn't shown, right-click on the picture and select Show Picture Toolbar from the menu.

 3. Click on the Crop button on the Picture toolbar. The mouse pointer turns into a cropping tool. (See Figure 16.5.)

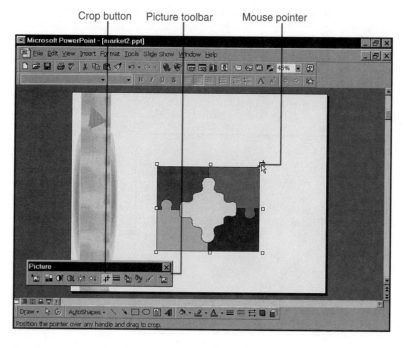

FIGURE 16.5   Use the cropping tool to chop off a section of the picture.

4. Move the mouse pointer over one of the handles. (Use a corner handle to crop two sides at once. Use a side, top, or bottom handle to crop only one side.)

5. Hold down the mouse button, and drag the pointer until the crop lines are where you want them.

6. Release the mouse button. The cropped section disappears.

TIP   **Uncropping**   You can uncrop a picture immediately after cropping it by selecting Edit, Undo or clicking the Undo button on the toolbar. You can also uncrop at any time, by performing the previous steps and dragging the selected handle in the opposite direction you dragged it for cropping.

In this lesson, you learned how to select, copy, move, rotate, and resize an object on a slide. In the next lesson, you will learn how to change the lines and colors of an object.

CHANGING THE LOOK OF AN OBJECT

In this lesson, you will learn how to add borders, colors, patterns, shadows, and 3-D effects to objects.

CHANGING LINE THICKNESS AND COLOR

In Lesson 14, you learned to draw your own artwork on a slide, and in Lesson 15, you learned to import clip art and other graphics. You can change the appearance of both kinds of artwork by modifying the colors and lines, but the procedures are different depending on whether the art is pre-drawn (a file you have imported) or drawn by you with the PowerPoint drawing tools.

 Drawing versus Picture In PowerPoint terms, a drawing is artwork that you have created yourself using PowerPoint's drawing tools, while a picture is artwork that you have imported in (such as clip art). If you want to change an imported picture's colors, see the section "Changing the Colors of a Picture" later in this lesson.

CHANGING A DRAWING'S COLORS AND LINES

If the line or shape you draw is not the color you expect it to be, you can change it. With lines, you have only one color option: change the line. With shapes, you can change the color of both the inside (fill) and the outside border (line).

Follow these steps to change the lines and/or color of any object you've drawn:

1. Right-click on the drawn object. A shortcut menu appears.

2. From the shortcut menu, select Format AutoShape, and then click on the Colors and Lines tab (see Figure 17.1).

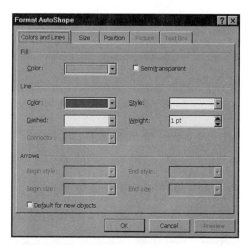

FIGURE 17.1   Use the Colors and Lines tab of the Format AutoShape dialog box to change the lines and colors for a drawn object.

 I Don't See Format AutoShape on the Menu!   If you right-click on a piece of clip art or other imported graphic, rather than one you've drawn yourself, you won't find the Format AutoShape command. However, you can select Format Picture instead and modify the picture's properties as explained in "Changing the Colors of a Picture" later in this lesson.

3. In the Fill section, open the Color list and select a different color for the inside of the shape. (This isn't applicable if the drawn object you're formatting is a line.)

For more color choices, choose More Colors and select from the dialog box that appears.

Textures and Patterns   From the Fill Color button, you can select Fill Effects. This opens a dialog box from which you can choose textures, patterns and gradients. Some textures are really cool—they look like wood, marble, or granite.

Semitransparent?   If you want to partially see through a shape to whatever is behind it, click the Semitransparent check box. For example, if you have a blue shape on a red background and you make the blue shape semi-transparent, it appears to be made up equally of red and blue. If you put the same shape on a white background, the shape appears light blue—a mixture of blue and white.

4. In the Line section, open the Color drop-down list and choose a line color. For shapes, the Line setting affects the color of the shape's outside border.

5. Choose a line style from the Style drop-down list. You can choose thick or thin lines, double lines, and so on.

6. If you want a different thickness, change the number in the Weight text box to a higher or lower number. (Measurements are in points. A point is 1/72 of an inch.)

7. If you want the line to be dashed (broken), choose a dash style from the Dashed drop-down list.

8. If you want arrows at one or both ends of a line, choose the beginning and ending arrow styles from the Arrows drop-down list. These controls will be unavailable if you are formatting a shape rather than a line.

9. If you want to draw all objects with these colors and line styles, you can specify them as the default by clicking the Default for New Objects check box.

10. Click OK. PowerPoint applies your changes to the shape.

 Changing the Entire Color Scheme If you want to change the entire color scheme for the presentation, don't mess around with individual objects—go straight to Lesson 18 for instructions.

CHANGING THE COLORS OF A PICTURE

When you paste a clip art image or insert a picture on a slide, the picture appears in its original colors. These colors may clash with the colors in your presentation. To change the colors in a picture, perform the following steps:

1. Click on the picture you want to change. A selection box appears around the picture.

2. Do either of the following to open the Recolor Picture dialog box shown in Figure 17.2.

  • If the Picture toolbar is not displayed, right-click the picture and select Show Picture Toolbar. Then click the Recolor Picture button on that toolbar.

  • Select Format, Colors and Lines. The Format Picture dialog box appears. Click on the Picture tab, and then the Recolor button.

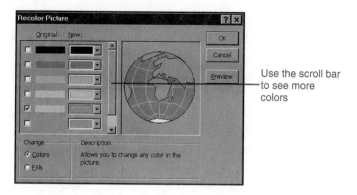

Use the scroll bar to see more colors

FIGURE 17.2 Use the Recolor Picture dialog box to change the colors in a picture.

3. In the Change area, select Colors to change line colors, or Fills to change colors between the lines.

Fills Isn't an Option!   With some picture types, Fills will be unavailable to select. That's okay—go ahead and select the colors, and the filled-in areas in the picture should change just fine.

4. Select a color you want to change in the Original list. A check mark appears in the check box next to the color.

5. Use the New drop-down menu to the right of the selected color to choose the color you want.

Using the Other Option   At the bottom of each color's **TIP** drop-down menu is the Other option. Select this option if you want to use a color that is not listed on the menu.

6. Repeat steps 3 through 5 for each color you want to change.

7. If you want to revert to an original color, remove the check mark from beside it.

8. Click OK to put your changes into effect.

DRAWING A BORDER AROUND A PICTURE

You can frame any object (a picture, a text box, or whatever) by drawing a border around the object. (This is the same as changing the line style and thickness on a drawn object.)

To add a border to an object, perform the following steps in Slide view:

1. Select the object you want to frame with a border, such as a text box or clip art object.

2. Choose Format, Colors and Lines. A dialog box appears that's appropriate for the type of object you selected (for instance, Format Text Box for a text box) with the Colors and Lines tab on top, as shown in Figure 17.1.

3. Open the Color drop-down list and choose a color for the line.

4. Open the Style drop-down list and choose a thickness and style for the line.

5. If you want the line to be dotted or dashed, open the Dashed drop-down list and choose a dash style.

6. Click OK. The border appears around the object.

ADDING A SHADOW OR A 3-D EFFECT

A shadow gives some depth to an object. Applying a 3-D effect to an object does much the same thing, as you can see in Figure 17.3. The main difference is that a shadow just adds shading behind a two-dimensional object, while a 3-D effect attempts to make the object appear fully three-dimensional. Shadows work with all objects, but 3-D effects work only with drawn artwork.

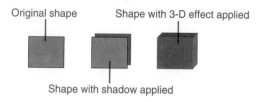

Original shape

Shape with 3-D effect applied

Shape with shadow applied

FIGURE 17.3 Shadows and 3-D effects can keep your artwork from looking flat and boring.

ADDING A SHADOW

To add a shadow to an object, perform these steps:

1. Select the object to which you want to add a shadow.

2. Click the Shadow tool on the Drawing toolbar. A menu of shadow options appears (see Figure 17.4).

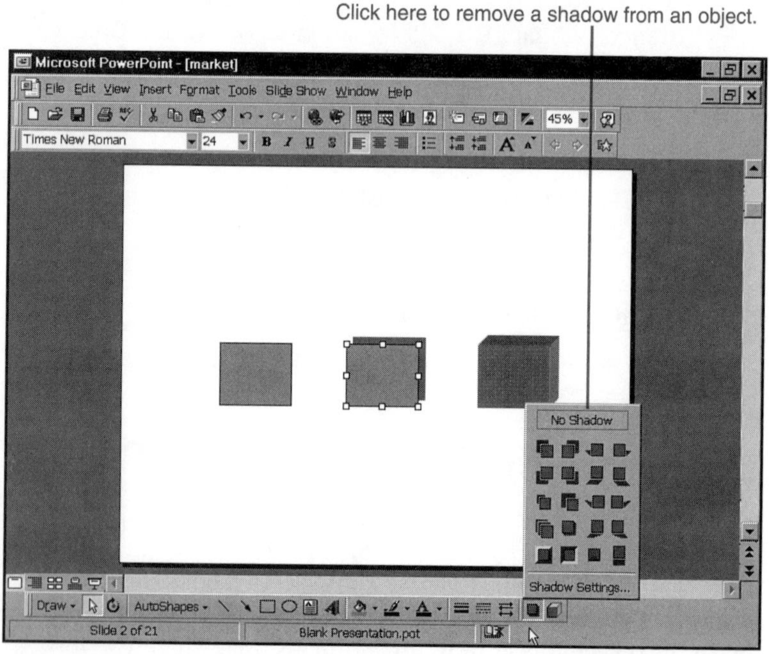

Click here to remove a shadow from an object.

FIGURE 17.4 Click on the type of shadow you want to use.

3. Click the type of shadow you want. The shadow is applied to the object.

4. (Optional) To make fine adjustments to the shadow, click the Shadow tool again and select Shadow Settings, then use the Shadow toolbar that appears:

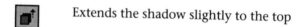 Toggles the shadow on/off

Extends the shadow slightly to the top

Extends the shadow slightly to the bottom

Extends the shadow slightly to the left

Extends the shadow slightly to the right

Changes the shadow color

ADDING A 3-D EFFECT

3-D effects are new for PowerPoint 97. They function like shadows, but they add more of a full three-dimensional look, as shown in Figure 17.3.

Follow these steps to apply a 3-D effect to an object:

1. Select the object. It must be an object you've drawn with the Drawing toolbar tools, not an imported piece of clip art.

2. Click the 3-D button on the Drawing toolbar. The 3-D tools appear (see Figure 17.5).

FIGURE 17.5 These 3-D tools enable you to apply a variety of special 3-D effects to a drawn object.

3. Click the 3-D effect that you want.

4. (Optional) Click the 3-D button again, and choose 3-D Settings, then use the 3-D toolbar that appears:

Toggles between 3-D and regular (2-D)

Tilt down

Tilt up

Tilt left

Tilt right

Adjust depth

Adjust direction

Adjust lighting

Change surface

Change color

COPYING THE LOOK OF ANOTHER OBJECT

If your presentation contains an object that has the frame, fill, and shadow you want to use for another object, you can pick up those design elements and apply them to another object. To do this, perform the following steps:

1. Click on the object with the style you want to copy.

 2. Click the Format Painter button on the Standard toolbar. PowerPoint copies the style.

3. Click on the object to which you want to apply the style. PowerPoint applies the copied style to the new object.

In this lesson, you learned how to use borders, colors, shadows, and 3-D effects to change the look of individual objects on a slide. You also learned how to copy design elements from object to object. In the next lesson, you will learn how to change the background colors and designs that appear on every slide in the presentation.

18

WORKING WITH PRESENTATION COLORS AND BACKGROUNDS

In this lesson, you will learn how to change the color scheme and background design of a presentation.

UNDERSTANDING COLOR SCHEMES AND BACKGROUNDS

Color schemes are sets of professionally selected complementary colors that you can use as the primary colors of a presentation. Each color scheme controls the color of the background, lines, text, shadows, fills, and other items on a slide. Using one of these color schemes ensures that your presentation looks appealing and professional.

Backgrounds are designs that control the way color appears on a slide. For example, you can select a background that spreads the color out from the upper-left corner to the edges.

You can select a color scheme and background for the Slide Master (which controls all the slides in the presentation), for the current slide, or for all slides in the presentation (thus overriding the Slide Master). Also, you can change individual colors in a color scheme to customize it.

SELECTING A COLOR SCHEME

The basic color scheme of your presentation depends on the active design template. You learned how to change design templates in Lesson 8—just select Format, Apply Design. Design templates include both color schemes and backgrounds.

Within each design template, there are several variations of one color scheme. All the color schemes in a template use the same basic colors, but each color scheme arranges its colors differently. For example, for on-screen viewing, the color scheme is a dark background and light text; for printing on a color printer, a light background and dark text; and, for printing on a one-color printer, a black-and-white color scheme.

You can select a color scheme for one slide or for all the slides in your presentation. To select a color scheme, perform the following steps:

1. If you don't want to change all the slides in the presentation, display or select the slide(s) with the color scheme you want to change.

2. Choose Format, Slide Color Scheme. The Color Scheme dialog box appears.

3. Click the Standard tab if it's not displayed. The color schemes available for the current design template appear (see Figure 18.1).

FIGURE 18.1   You can choose a standard color scheme from the ones the current template offers.

4. Click one of the color schemes, and click Apply to apply it to the selected slides or Apply All to apply it to all slides in the presentation.

CUSTOMIZING A COLOR SCHEME

Even though each template comes with its own color scheme, you can customize the scheme for a presentation. You can adjust individual colors, or radically change them all.

 Stay Consistent Be careful when you change the colors on a single slide. You don't want one slide to clash with the rest of your slides.

1. If you don't want to change all the slides in the presentation, display or select the slide with the color scheme you want to change.

2. Choose Format, Slide Color Scheme. The Color Scheme dialog box appears.

3. Click the Custom tab. The dialog box changes, as shown in Figure 18.2.

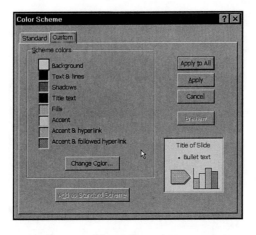

FIGURE 18.2 You can change individual colors in a scheme with the Custom tab.

4. Click on one of the colors (for example, Background), and click the Change Color button. A dialog box appears that enables you to select a new color. For example, the Background Color dialog box is shown in Figure 18.3.

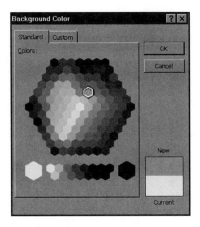

FIGURE 18.3   Each on-screen element has its own dialog box for customizing its color.

5. To select a color, click the Standard tab, click on any color you see, and click OK. To create a new color, click the Custom tab, use the controls to custom select a color, and click OK.

 TIP   **Custom Controls**   Most beginners use the Standard tab in step 5. There are enough colors shown there to suit most purposes. With the custom controls, you can fine-tune a color's hue, saturation, and luminescence, and adjust its red, green, and blue tones numerically.

6. Repeat steps 4 and 5 for each color you want to change.

7. Click Apply to All to apply the new colors to every slide in the presentation, or click Apply to apply them to only the current slide.

More Background Controls You can change the color of the background using the Format, Slide Color Scheme command, but if you want to change the texture or pattern of the background, or use a picture as a background, you need to use the Custom Background command, discussed later in this lesson.

COPYING A SLIDE'S COLOR SCHEME TO ANOTHER SLIDE

If you want to change the color scheme for an entire presentation, it's best to make the changes to the Slide Master. However, if you want to change several slides, but not all of them, you can make the changes to a single slide, and copy that slide's color scheme to the others. Follow these steps to copy a slide's color scheme:

1. Display your presentation in Slide Sorter view.

2. Select the slide containing the color scheme you want to copy.

 3. Click the Format Painter button on the toolbar.

4. Click on the slide that you want to receive the color scheme.

5. Repeat the process to recolor each slide you want to change.

CHANGING THE BACKGROUND DESIGN

An effective background adds a professional look to any presentation. PowerPoint enables you to set the background to any color, and to add patterns, textures, and shadings to it.

PowerPoint on the Web   If you are creating a presentation for use on the Web, try to keep the background light-colored. It will be easier for your readers to view on their monitors this way. Save dark backgrounds for slides designed to be shown on large screens.

To change the background for your presentation or to modify the existing background, perform the following steps:

1. Display or select the slide with the background you want to change. To change the slide backgrounds in the entire presentation, display the Slide Master.

2. Choose Format, Background or right-click on the background and select Background from the shortcut menu. The Background dialog box appears.

3. Open the drop-down list under Background Fill (see Figure 18.4).

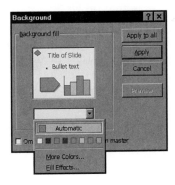

FIGURE 18.4   Choose a color from the ones shown, or click More Colors or Fill Effects.

4. Click on one of the following options:

   • Automatic sets the background to whatever the Slide Master currently shows as the background.

   • A solid color sets the background to that color.

- More Colors opens a Colors dialog box similar to the one shown in Figure 18.3, in which you can choose from a color assortment.

- Fill Effects opens a dialog box in which you can choose many special effects like a gradient fill, textured backgrounds, or pictures used as backgrounds.

 Gradient Fill   A gradient is where the background starts out one color at the top of the slide and gradually changes to another color. When one of those colors is white (or in some schemes black), it's known as a one-color gradient. When neither color is white (or black), it's a two-color gradient.

5. Click on Apply to apply the background only to this slide, or click on Apply To All to apply the background to all the slides in the presentation.

In this lesson, you learned how to select and modify a color scheme, and how to copy a color scheme from one presentation to another. You also learned how to change the background color and design for a slide or presentation. In the next lesson, you will learn how to add a graph to a slide.

ADDING A GRAPH TO A SLIDE

19

*In this lesson, you will learn how to create a graph
(or chart) and place it on a presentation slide.*

INSERTING A GRAPH

PowerPoint comes with a program called Microsoft Graph that
transforms raw data into professional-looking graphs. To create a
graph, perform the following steps:

1. Display the slide to which you want to add the graph.

2. Click on the Insert Chart button on the Standard toolbar,
   or select Insert, Chart. The Microsoft Graph window appears. In Figure 19.1, the Datasheet window is up front.

Datasheet The datasheet is set up like a spreadsheet
with rows, columns, and cells. Each rectangle in the
datasheet is a cell that can hold text or numbers.
Microsoft Graph converts the data you enter in the
datasheet into a graph it displays in the Graph window.

3. First, you change the datasheet values to your own
   figures. Click inside the cell that contains a label or value
   you want to change, and type your entry.

4. Click on the next cell you want to change, or use the
   arrow keys to move from cell to cell.

5. Repeat steps 3 and 4 until you enter all your data.

6. Click on the graph. The datasheet window disappears,
   and the graph appears.

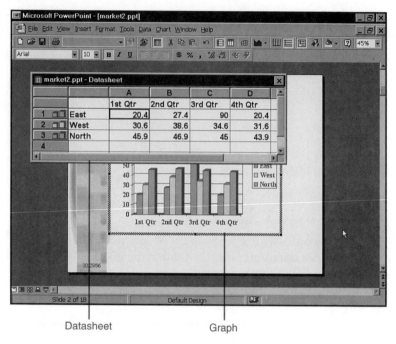

Datasheet   Graph

FIGURE 19.1 The Datasheet window appears in the front.

7. To leave Microsoft Graph and return to your slide in PowerPoint, click anywhere outside the graph.

TIP   **Redisplaying the Datasheet** If you need to make a change in the datasheet after you create it, see the next section, "Editing the Datasheet."

TIP   **Moving and Resizing the Graph** If the graph is too big or is in a bad location on the slide, you can resize and move it. Refer to Lesson 20 for details.

EDITING THE DATASHEET

If you return to your slide and later decide that you want to edit the data that your graph is based on, perform the following steps:

1. Display the slide that contains the graph you want to edit.

2. Double-click anywhere inside the graph. PowerPoint starts Microsoft Graph and displays the graph.

 3. If Microsoft Graph does not display the Datasheet window, choose View, Datasheet or click the View Datasheet button in the Microsoft Graph toolbar. The Datasheet window appears.

4. Use the Tab key to go to the cell that contains the value you want to change, and type your change.

5. When you are done, click anywhere inside the graph window.

In addition to editing individual data entries, you can cut, copy, and paste cells; delete and insert rows and columns; and adjust column widths. This list gives you a quick overview of how to edit your datasheet:

Selecting Cells   To select one cell, click on it. To select several cells, drag the mouse pointer over the desired cells. To select a row or column, click on the letter above the column or the number to the left of the row. To select all the cells, click on the upper-leftmost square in the datasheet.

Clearing Cells   To erase the contents of cells, select the cells, and select Edit, Clear. Select All (to clear contents and formatting), Contents (to remove only the contents), or Formats (to remove only the formatting). You can also just press the Delete key to clear the contents (not the for-matting), or right-click and choose Clear Contents.

Cutting or Copying Cells   To cut cells, select the cells you want to cut. Then select Edit, Cut, or click on the Cut button. To copy cells, select the cells you want to copy.

Then select Edit, Copy, or click on the Copy button. You also can right-click and select Cut or Copy from the shortcut menu instead.

Pasting Cells   To paste copied or cut cells into a datasheet, select the cell in the upper-left corner of the area in which you want to paste the cut or copied cells. Select Edit, Paste, or click on the Paste button. You also can right-click on the destination area and select Paste from the shortcut menu.

Inserting Blank Cells   To insert blank cells into your datasheet, select the row, column, or number of cells you want to insert. (Rows will be inserted above the current row. Columns will be inserted to the left of the current column.) Select Insert, Cells. If you select a row or column, PowerPoint inserts the row or column. If you select one or more cells, the Insert Cells dialog box appears, asking if you want to shift surrounding cells down or to the right. Select your preference, and click on the OK button. As a shortcut, you can right-click where you want the cells to go and select Insert from the shortcut menu.

Changing the Column Width   If you type entries that are too wide for a particular column, you may want to adjust the column width. Move the mouse pointer over the column letter at the top of the column you want to change. Move the mouse pointer to the right until it turns into a double-headed arrow. Hold down the mouse button and drag the mouse until the column is the desired width.

Changing the Data Series

Say you create a graph that shows the sales figures for several salespersons over four quarters. You wanted each column in the graph to represent a salesperson, but instead, the columns represent quarters. To fix the graph, you can swap the data series by performing the following steps:

1. Open the Data menu.

2. Select Series in Rows or Series in Columns.

> **Quick Data Series Swap**   To quickly swap data series,
> **TIP**   click on the By Row or By Column button on the Standard
> toolbar.

CHANGING THE CHART TYPE

By default, Microsoft Graph creates a three-dimensional column
chart. If you want Microsoft Graph to display your data in a
different type of chart, perform the following steps:

1. Choose Chart, Chart Type. The Chart Type dialog box
   appears, as shown in Figure 19.2.

FIGURE 19.2   Pick the chart type you want.

2. Click on the desired chart type from the Chart Type area.

3. Click on a sub-type from the Chart Sub-type area. The
   sub-types change depending on what type you chose in
   step 2.

4. (Optional) To view a sample before you accept the chart, click and hold down the mouse button on the Press and Hold to View Sample button.

5. (Optional) To make this type of chart the default, click the Set as default chart button.

6. Click OK.

Quick Change To quickly change the chart type, click the Chart Type button on the toolbar and select from a drop-down list of chart types that appears.

PowerPoint on the Web If you are designing a chart for Web viewing, keep it as simple and self-explanatory as possible, avoiding the more complicated chart types. Keep in mind that there will not be a narrator presenting the slide show who can explain what the chart means; the reader will need to be able to understand it on his own.

Applying Custom Chart Types

Microsoft Graph comes with several predesigned chart formats that you can apply to your chart. You select the custom chart type you want, and Microsoft Graph reformats your chart, giving it a professional look. Here's how you use Custom Chart Types to select a chart design:

1. Choose Chart, Chart Type. The Chart Type dialog box appears, as shown in Figure 19.2.

2. Click the Custom Types tab. The display changes to the one shown in Figure 19.3.

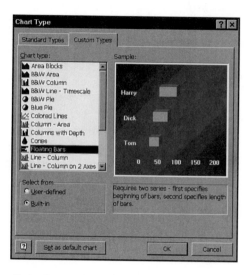

FIGURE 19.3   Select a custom chart type using the Custom Types tab.

3. From the Chart Type list, choose a chart type. In the Sample area, Microsoft Graph creates a sample of the selected chart type.

4. Click OK. Microsoft Graph reformats the chart using the selected custom type.

In this lesson, you learned how to create and insert graphs on a slide, enter and edit graph data, and change graph types. In the next lesson, you will learn how to enhance graphs.

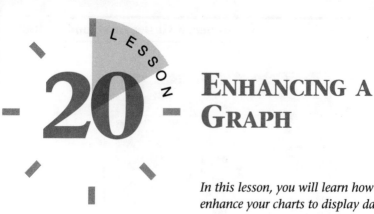

LESSON 20

ENHANCING A GRAPH

In this lesson, you will learn how to enhance your charts to display data more clearly and more attractively.

WHAT CAN YOU ADD TO A CHART?

You can format existing elements and add elements to a chart to enhance it. Here's a list of some of the more common enhancements:

- **Fonts**   You can specify type style, size, and attributes for the text you use in the chart.

- **Colors**   You can change the color of text, lines, bars, and pie slices that you use in your charts to represent data.

- **Axes**   You can display or hide the lines of the X and Y axes.

- **Titles and Labels**   You can add a title to the chart or add labels for any of the axes or data points.

Axes   Axes is the plural of axis. The Y axis is the line that runs up the left side of the chart. This axis has the chart values on it. The X axis is the line that runs across the bottom of the chart. This axis has the data series on it. In a 3-D object, you have a third axis: It's Z, and it measures the depth, or "front-to-back" distance of a 3-D object.

- **Text Boxes**   You can add explanatory text or other text in a separate box.

- **Borders and Shading**   You can add a border around a chart or add background shading to a chart.

Chart or Graph? PowerPoint uses these two terms interchangeably. You use the Insert Chart command to add a chart, but Microsoft Graph is the program that does the work. Don't worry about making a distinction between the two.

DISPLAYING THE CHART IN MICROSOFT GRAPH

Before you can enhance an existing chart, you must display it in Microsoft Graph. Perform the following steps:

1. In Slide view, display the slide that contains the graph you want to enhance.

2. Click on the graph to select it. A selection box appears around the graph.

3. Select Edit, Chart Object, Edit or double-click the graph. PowerPoint starts Microsoft Graph and displays the graph.

Text Boxes and Lines You can add text boxes, lines, arrows, and basic shapes to graphs in much the same way you can add them to slides. To display the Drawing toolbar, right-click on the Standard toolbar and select Drawing. Refer to Lesson 14 for details on drawing.

PARTS OF A CHART

Before you start adding enhancements to a chart, you should understand that a chart is made up of several objects. By clicking on an object, you make it active, and handles appear around it, as shown in Figure 20.1. You can then move or resize the object or change its appearance, by doing any of the following:

- Double-click on an object to display a dialog box that enables you to change the object's appearance. For example, if you double-click on a column in a column chart, you can change its color.

- Right-click on the object, and select the desired formatting option from the shortcut menu.

- Select the object, and select an option from the Format or Insert menu. The Format menu helps you change the appearance of the object; the Insert menu enables you to add objects to a chart, including a legend, data labels, and a chart title.

The following sections tell you how to add some commonly used enhancements to a chart.

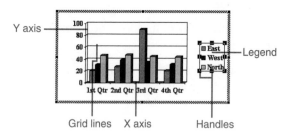

Figure 20.1   Each chart consists of several individual objects.

Adding a Title

You add various titles to a chart to help indicate what the chart is all about. You can add a chart title that appears at the top of the chart, and you can add axis titles that appear along the X and Y axes. Here's how you add titles and labels to a chart:

1. Select Chart, Chart Options, or right-click on the chart and choose Chart Options.

2. Click the Titles tab if it is not already displayed.

3. Enter the title you want in the Chart Title text box.

4. If you want titles for the X, Y, and/or Z axes, enter them in the appropriate text boxes (X, Y, or Z).

5. Click OK. Microsoft Graph returns you to the chart window with your new titles in place.

FORMATTING TEXT ON A CHART

PowerPoint inserts any text you add to a chart into a text box. To format text on a chart, perform these steps:

1. Right-click on the text that you want to format. A shortcut menu appears.

2. Select the Format option. The Format option's exact name differs depending on the object. If you right-click on the chart title, the option reads Format Chart Title.

3. Enter your preferences in the Format dialog box. This dialog box typically contains tabs for Pattern, Font, and Alignment, but you may not see all of these, depending on the text type.

4. Click OK when you finish.

FORMATTING THE AXES

You can enhance the X and Y axes in a number of ways, including changing the font of the text, scaling the axes, and changing the number format.

Here's how you change the axis formatting:

1. Right-click on the axis you want to format and choose Format Axis, or click on the axis, open the Format menu, and choose Selected Axis. The Format Axis dialog box appears, as shown in Figure 20.2.

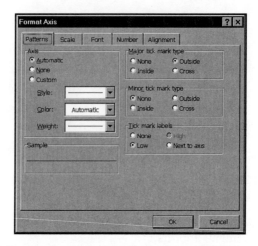

Figure 20.2   The Format Axis dialog box enables you to change the look of the axis and its text.

2. Enter your preferences in the dialog box. There are several tabs containing different formatting options.

3. Click OK or press Enter when you finish.

Enhancing the Chart Frame

You can change the overall look of a chart by adding a border or shading. Follow these steps to add a border or shading:

1. Click on the chart anywhere outside a specific chart object. Handles appear around the entire chart.

2. Select Format, Selected Chart Area, or right-click on the chart and choose Format Chart Area. The Format Chart Area dialog box appears.

3. Enter your border and color preferences, and click OK.

Changing the Look of 3-D Charts

3-D charts are very attractive, but they're also a bit tricky to format. To make the various 3-D elements stand out, you may want to tilt the chart or rotate it. Here's how to format a 3-D chart:

1. Choose Chart, 3-D View. The 3-D View dialog box appears, as shown in Figure 20.3. As you make changes, a wire-frame picture in the middle of the dialog box reflects the changes.

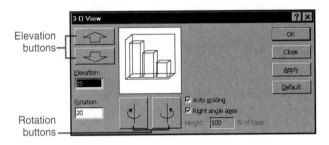

Elevation buttons
Rotation buttons

FIGURE 20.3 Changing the 3-D view.

2. To change the elevation (the height from which you see the chart), click on the up or down elevation buttons, or type a number in the Elevation box.

3. To change the rotation (the rotation around the Z-axis), click on the left or right rotation buttons, or type a number in the Rotation box.

4. If there is a perspective option, you can change the perspective (perceived depth) by clicking on the up or down perspective controls, or typing a number in the Perspective box. Not all charts have this control.

5. To see the proposed changes on the actual chart, click on the Apply button.

6. When you are done making changes, click OK, or press Enter.

In this lesson, you learned how to improve the appearance of your chart. In the next lesson, you will learn how to add an organizational chart to a slide.

21 ADDING AN ORGANIZATIONAL CHART

In this lesson, you will learn how to add an organizational chart to a slide and how to edit the chart.

INSERTING AN ORGANIZATIONAL CHART

PowerPoint comes with Microsoft Organization Chart, a program that can create organizational charts to show the management structure in a company, a family tree, or relationships among any objects. To create and place an organizational chart on a slide, perform the following steps:

1. Display the slide on which you want to place the organizational chart.

2. Select Insert, Picture, Organization Chart. The Microsoft Organization Chart window appears.

3. If the Microsoft Organization Chart window is too small, click on the Maximize button in the upper-right corner of the window to make it full-screen size.

4. Click on a box in the chart, and type the name, title, and up to two optional comments about the person in the organization. Press Enter to start a new line after typing each item. Press Esc when you complete the entry for that person.

5. Repeat step 4 for each person you want to include in the organizational chart.

6. To add another box to the chart, click on the appropriate button at the top of the screen (see Figure 21.1). Then click on the box to which you want to connect the new box. The new box appears. Figure 21.1 shows a chart with several boxes, including three subordinate boxes added to the default boxes.

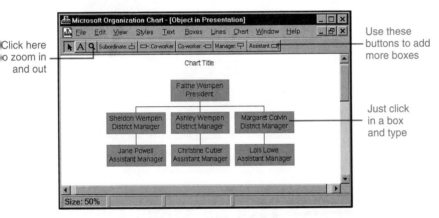

FIGURE 21.1   Type your entries into the basic structure to form a chart.

7. To return to your slide and insert the organizational chart on it, select File, Exit and Return to *filename* or click the MS Organization Chart window's Close (X) button. If asked if you want to update the image, click on the Yes button. The organization chart appears on the slide.

PowerPoint on the Web   Check with management before publishing your company's organizational chart on a public Web server. Some companies consider their organization sensitive information and do not want it shared with competitors and other outsiders.

Editing an Organizational Chart

Before you can edit an existing organizational chart, you must restart MS Organization Chart. To restart the program, perform the following steps:

1. In Slide view, display the slide that contains the organizational chart you want to edit.

2. Double-click on the organizational chart. MS Organization Chart reopens, displaying the chart for editing.

 Zoom In As you work on the chart, you can zoom in or out to see more or less of the chart at once. Just open the View menu and select a different view (for instance, 50% of Actual is the default) or press one of the corresponding shortcut keys (F9 through F12). To quickly view the chart at Actual Size, click the magnifying glass button.

Selecting One or More Levels

As you edit, add to, or enhance an organizational chart, you need to select the boxes with which you want to work. This list explains how to select one or more boxes or levels:

- To select a single box, click on it. To move from one box to another, use the arrow keys.

- To select more than one box, hold down the Shift key while clicking on each box.

- To select a specific group of boxes (for example, all manager boxes), choose Edit, Select, and click on the desired group.

- To select a specific level in the organization, choose Edit, Select Levels, and type the range of levels you want to select (for example, 2 through 5).

CUTTING, COPYING, AND PASTING BOXES

To rearrange your organizational chart, you can cut, copy, and paste boxes. To move or copy boxes, perform the following steps:

1. Select the box or boxes you want to copy or move. Hold down Shift as you select to select more than one.

2. Select Edit, Cut (to remove the boxes), or Edit, Copy (to copy them). Alternatively, you can right-click on them and select Copy or Cut from the shortcut menu.

3. Select the box to which you want to attach the copied or cut boxes.

4. Select Edit, Paste Boxes. This action pastes the boxes to the right of or below the selected box.

Undoing Cut or Paste   You can undo any operation immediately after performing it by selecting Edit, Undo. However, in MS Organization Chart, you can undo only the most recent action.

SELECTING A CHART STYLE

The chart you create resembles a family tree. If that structure does not suit your needs (for all or part of the chart), you can change the structure. To select a style for your organizational chart, follow these steps:

1. Select the boxes to which you want to apply the new style. To apply your changes to the entire chart, select all the boxes.

2. Open the Styles menu, and click on the desired style (see Figure 21.2). Microsoft Organization Chart applies the specified style to the selected boxes.

Select a
structure for
part or all of
the chart.

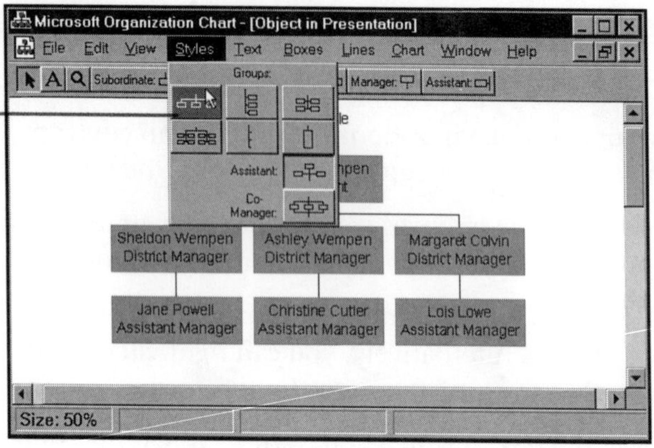

FIGURE 21.2   Use the Styles menu to restructure your chart.

FORMATTING THE TEXT

You may want to use a different font, type style, type size, or
color for a person's name and position, or for different levels in
the chart. Or you may want to change the text alignment in the
box from center to left or right. To format the text in a box, do
the following:

1. Select the text you want to format:

   • Click on a box to format all the text in the box.

   • To format part of the text in a box, drag over the
     desired text.

   • Hold down the Shift key, and click on two or more
     boxes to format the text in every selected box.

2. Select Text, Font. The Font dialog box appears.

3. Change one or more of the following options:

   • Font   Select a typeface from the Font list.

   • Font Style   Select a style (for example, bold or italic)
     from the Font Style list.

   • Size   Select a type size (in points) from the Size list.

What about Script?   The Font dialog box has a Script drop-down list in it too. The Script option enables you to select the alphabet characters you use for a particular language. The default is Western, which means most English-speaking languages. You might also have Turkish and Central European to choose from here, for typing in those languages. If you bought your copy of PowerPoint in an English-speaking country, you probably have only Western on the list.

4. Click OK.

5. To change the color of the text, select Text, Color, and click on the desired color in the dialog box that appears.

6. To change the alignment of the text in the box, open the Text menu, and select Left, Right, or Center.

CHANGING THE LOOK OF THE BOXES AND LINES

Microsoft Organization Chart formats the boxes and lines that make up an organizational chart for you. However, you can change the attributes of either boxes or lines. Follow these steps to format boxes or lines:

1. Select the boxes you want to format. You select lines by clicking on them.

2. Open the Boxes menu, and select the desired option: Shadow, Border Style, or Border Line Style. Or, open the Lines menu, and select either Thickness or Style.

3. A submenu opens, providing you with a list of available settings. Click on a setting, and Microsoft Organization Chart applies it to the selection.

Another way to change border settings, is to right click on the selected box and select the attribute you want to change from the shortcut menu.

You can also change the color of a line or box by selecting Line, Color or Box, Color. (You change the box's border color by selecting Box, Border Color.) A dialog box opens in which you choose a new color.

 Returning to Your Slide   When you finish editing and enhancing your organizational chart, you can return to your slide by selecting File, Exit and Return to *filename* or click the Close (X) button on the MS Organization Chart window. Click on the Yes button to update your changes.

In this lesson, you learned how to create, edit, and enhance an organizational chart. In the next lesson, you will learn how to view a slide show, make basic movements within a presentation, and create action buttons.

VIEWING A
SLIDE SHOW

LESSON

22

In this lesson, you will learn how to view a slide show on-screen, make basic movements within a presentation, and create action buttons that let you (or another user) control the action.

Before you take your presentation "on the road" to show to your intended audience, you should run through it several times on your own computer, checking that all the slides are in the right order and that the timings and transitions between the slides work correctly. You can set up a slide show to run itself—that is, with a certain amount of time elapsing between each slide—or manually, with or without on-screen controls.

This lesson covers basic movement within a presentation—from Slide A to Slide B to Slide C and so on. In Lesson 23, you'll learn about transition effects you can add that make the movement from slide to slide more visually interesting.

VIEWING AN ON-SCREEN SLIDE SHOW

You can preview a slide show at any time to see how the show looks to your audience. To view a slide show, perform the following steps:

1. Open the presentation you want to view.

2. Click the Slide Show button at the bottom of the presentation window. The first slide in the presentation appears full-screen.

3. To display the next or previous slide, do one of the following:

    *   To display the next slide, click the left mouse button press the Page Down key, or press the right arrow or down arrow key.

- To display the previous slide, click the right mouse button, press the Page Up key, or click on the left arrow or up arrow key.

- To quit the slide show, press the Esc key.

 Start the Show! Clicking the Slide Show button is the fastest way to start a slide show. Other ways to start a slide show include selecting View, Slide Show and selecting Slide Show, View Show.

CONTROLLING THE SLIDE SHOW

While you view a slide show, you can do more than just move from slide to slide. When you move your mouse, notice the triangle in a box at the bottom left corner of the slide show (see Figure 22.1). Click on it for a pop-up menu that contains commands you can use as you actually give the presentation:

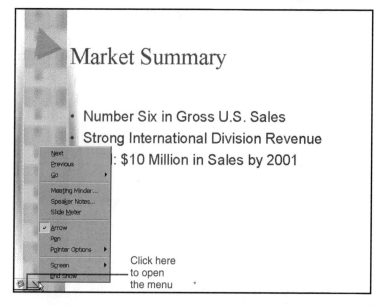

FIGURE 22.1 You can control the slide show while you present it with this menu.

- The Next and Previous commands enable you to move from slide to slide. (It's easier to change slides using other methods, though.)

- Choose Go, Slide Navigator to bring up a dialog box listing every slide in the presentation. You can jump quickly to any slide with it. You can also jump to a slide with a specific title (if you know it) by selecting Go, Title, and choosing the title from the list.

- Click Meeting Minder to bring up a window where you can take notes as the meeting associated with your presentation progresses.

- Choose Speaker Notes to view your notes for the slide.

- Choose Slide Meter to open a dialog box that enables you to control the timing between slides. (More about timing shortly.)

- Arrow and Pen are mouse options. Arrow is the default. Your mouse can serve as an arrow, to point out parts of the slide, or as a pen, to write comments on the slide or circle key areas, as you give your presentation. Keep in mind, however, that it is very difficult to write legibly using an ordinary mouse or trackball.

- Pointer Options enables you to choose a color for the pen, and whether to display or hide the pointer.

- Screen opens a submenu that enables you to pause the show, blank the screen, and erase any pen marks you made on the slide.

- End Show takes you back to PowerPoint's slide editing window.

SETTING SLIDE SHOW OPTIONS

Depending on the type of show you're presenting, you may find it useful to make some adjustments to the way the show runs, such as making it run in a window (the default is full-screen) or showing only certain slides. You'll find these controls and more in the Set Up Show dialog box (see Figure 22.2). To open it, choose Slide Show, Set Up Show.

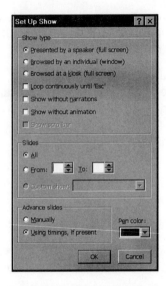

FIGURE 22.2   Use the Set Up Show dialog box to give PowerPoint some basic instructions about how to present your slide show.

In this dialog box, you can:

- Choose what medium the presentation is going to be shown in. Your choices are Presented by a speaker (full screen), Browsed by an individual (window), and Browsed at a kiosk (full screen).

- Choose whether to loop the slide show continuously or just show it once. You might want to loop it continuously if it were running unaided at a kiosk at a trade show, for instance.

- Show without narration, if you have created any. (You'll learn about narration later in this lesson.)

- Show without animation, if you have added any. (You'll learn about animation in Lesson 23.)

- Show all the slides or a range of them (which you enter in the From and To boxes).

- Choose a custom show, if you have created one. (To create a custom show, for instance one that contains a subset of the main show's slides, select Slide Show, Custom Show.)

- Choose whether to advance slides manually or using timings you set up. (You'll learn to add timings in Lesson 23.)

- Choose a pen color. (Remember, in Figure 22.1 there was a Pen option that made the mouse pointer turn into a pen? This is the same pen.)

ADDING ACTION BUTTONS ON SLIDES

In the preceding section, you saw how the Set Up Show dialog box enables you to choose between automatic and manual advance. In most cases, you will want to have the slides advance manually, since different people read at different speeds. Even if you are creating a presentation for a speaker to give, you will usually want manual advancing since you can't anticipate when the speaker may need extra time to answer a question.

As you saw at the beginning of this lesson, one way to advance or go back in a slide show is to press the Page Down key or Page Up key on the keyboard. This simple method works fine, except for two things:

- In a kiosk-type setting, you may not want the audience to have access to the computer's keyboard.

- This method simply plods from slide to slide, with no opportunity to jump to special slides or jump to the beginning or end quickly.

A new feature that solves this problem in PowerPoint 97 is the capability of adding action buttons to slides. Action buttons are like controls on an audio CD player—they let you jump to any slide quickly, go back, go forward, or even stop the presentation.

Same Controls on All Slides? If you want to add the same action buttons to all slides in the presentation, add the action buttons to the Slide Master. To display the Slide Master, select View, Master, Slide Master.

To add an action button to a slide, follow these steps:

1. Display the slide in Slide view.

2. Select Slide Show, Action Buttons, and pick a button from the palette that appears next to the command (see Figure 22.3). For instance, if you want to create a button that advances to the next slide, you might choose the button with the arrow pointing to the right.

Which Button Should I Choose? Choose any button you like; at this point you are only choosing a picture to show on the button, not any particular function for it. However, you might consider the action that you want the button to perform, and then pick a button picture that matches it well.

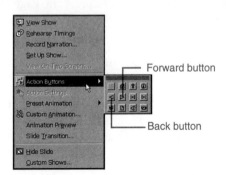

FIGURE 22.3 Choose the button that you think your reader will most strongly identify with the action you're going to assign to it.

3. Your mouse pointer turns into a crosshair. Drag to draw a
   box on the slide where you want the button to appear.
   (You can resize it later if you want, the same way you
   resized graphics in Lesson 16.) PowerPoint draws the
   button on the slide and opens the Action Settings dialog
   box (see Figure 22.4).

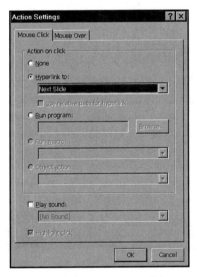

FIGURE 22.4   You can control the way one slide transitions to the
next with the Action Settings dialog box.

4. Choose the type of action you want to happen when the
   user clicks the button. Most of the time you will choose
   Hyperlink To, but your complete list of choices is:

   - None

   - Hyperlink To   This can be a slide, an Internet
     hyperlink, a document on your computer—just
     about anything.

   - Run Program   You can choose to have a program
     start when the user clicks on the button.

   - Run Macro   If you have recorded a macro, you can
     have the user run it from the button.

- If you have embedded (OLE) objects in the presentation, you can activate one when the button is clicked.

5. Open the drop-down list for the type of action you chose, and select the exact action (for instance, Next Slide). Or, if you chose Run Program, click the Browse button and locate the program to be run.

6. (Optional) If you want a sound to play when the user clicks on the button, select the Play Sound check box and choose a sound from the drop-down list.

7. (Optional) If you want it to look highlighted when the user clicks the button (a nice little extra), leave the Highlight Click check box marked.

8. Click OK. Your button appears on the slide.

9. View the presentation (as you learned at the beginning of this lesson) to try out the button.

Figure 22.5 shows three buttons added to a slide. Actually, they were added to the Slide Master, so the same buttons appear on each slide in the presentation. This kind of consistency gives the reader a feeling of comfort and control.

No Controls on Slide 1   When you add action buttons to the Slide Master, they appear on every slide except the first one in the presentation. If you want action buttons on the first slide, you must add them specifically to that slide or to the Title Master.

Don't Group   Each action button must be an independent object on the slide. Don't group them together or they won't work properly.

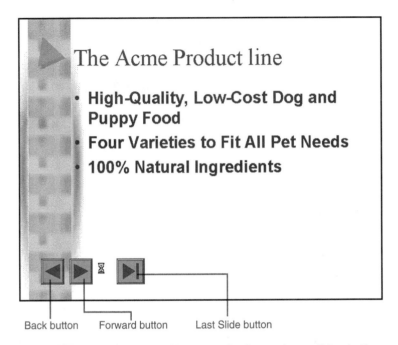

Back button   Forward button   Last Slide button

FIGURE 22.5   These control buttons display various slides in the presentation.

In this lesson you learned how to display a slide presentation on-screen, move between slides, and create buttons on the slides to control the movement. In the next lesson, you'll learn to set the timing and transitions between slides.

LESSON 23

TRANSITIONS, TIMING, AND ANIMATION

In this lesson, you will learn about transitions between slides and setting up automatic advances with specified timing.

An on-screen slide show is a lot like the slide show you put on using a slide projector. However, with an on-screen slide show, you can add impressive and professional visual effects (transitions and effects) that provide smooth and attention-getting movements from one slide or object to the next.

Transitions and Effects A transition is a way of moving from one slide to the next. For example, with a vertical blinds transition, the slide takes on the look of window blinds that turn to reveal the next slide. An effect is also an animated movement from one thing to another, but it pertains to individual objects on the slide, such as a bulleted list or a movie, rather than to the appearance or disappearance of the entire slide.

SETTING UP TRANSITIONS AND TIMING

Transitions and timing are actually two very different things, but they happen to be set using the same PowerPoint controls. A transition, as explained previously, is an animation that moves the presentation along from one slide to the next. The default transition is for one slide to simply vanish and the next slide appear in its place.

Setting timing is optional. The default timing is None, which means the speaker or audience must advance the slides manually (as you learned to do in Lesson 22). When you set timing for a transition between two slides, you are specifying the amount of time the first slide will appear on-screen before the next slide moves in to take its place.

Because transitions and timings are independent, you can set one or both for any slide individually.

To apply a slide transition and/or timing to a slide, perform the following steps:

1. Open the presentation to which you want to add transitions and/or timing.

2. Switch to Slide Sorter view. (Click on the Slide Sorter button.) The Slide Sorter toolbar appears at the top of the screen. (See Figure 23.1.)

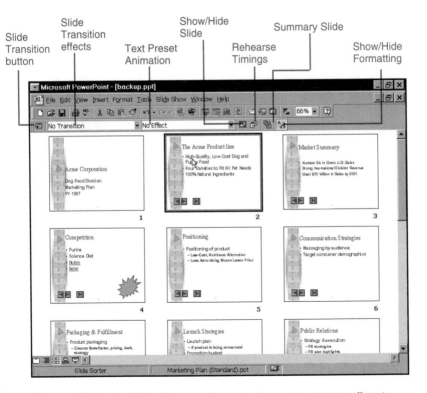

FIGURE 23.1 In Slide Sorter view, you have an extra toolbar to work with that controls transitions.

3. Select the slide to which you want to add a transition. To select more than one slide, hold down the Shift key as you select. To select all slides, press Ctrl+A.

4. Select Slide Show, Slide Transition, or click the Slide Transition button (shown in Figure 23.1). The Slide Transition dialog box appears, as shown in Figure 23.2.

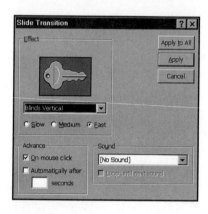

Figure 23.2   Use this dialog box to add transition effects and timing to the slides you select.

5. Open the Effect drop-down list and choose a transition effect. (Keep an eye on the preview area to see a demonstration of the effect.)

 Oops! I Missed It!   PowerPoint demonstrates a transition immediately on the picture in the dialog box when you select it. You can click on the picture to see the demonstration again if you miss it the first time.

6. At the bottom of the Effect area, select the desired speed for the transition to take effect: Slow, Medium, or Fast.

7. (Optional) To set a time for automatic slide advance, select one of the options in the Advance group:

- On Mouse Click moves from this slide to the next slide only when you click the mouse button or press an arrow key.

- Automatically After ____ Seconds moves automatically from slide to slide after the specified number of seconds.

8. To associate a sound with the transition, select one from the Sound drop-down list. (To loop the sound so that it plays over and over, select the Loop Until Next Sound check box.)

9. Click on the Apply button to apply the settings to the slide(s) you selected, or click Apply to All to apply the settings to all slides in the presentation.

Quick Transition Setup To quickly apply a transition (without timing), pull down the **Transitions** drop-down list on the Slide Sorter toolbar (see Figure 23.1) and select the desired transition.

ADDING ANIMATION EFFECTS

While transitions affect an entire slide, effects apply to individual elements on the slide. For instance, you might want the slide's background and title to appear first (using a transition), and then have the individual items on a bulleted list appear, one at a time, beneath the heading.

Animation When most people think of animation, they think of cartoons, but PowerPoint uses "animation" to mean the movement on-screen that acts as a transition from one object or slide to the next.

ANIMATING THE TEXT ON A SLIDE

The simplest form of animation is to animate the text on a slide separately from its title and background. When you choose one of these effects, the title and background appear as specified by the transition, and then the rest of the slide's text appears, paragraph by paragraph, using the chosen effect.

To apply simple animation effects to an object on a slide, follow these steps:

1. In Slide Sorter view, select the slide that contains the text you want to animate.

2. Open the Text Preset Animation drop-down list on the Slide Sorter toolbar and select an animation effect for the text on that slide.

 3. Switch to Slide Show view to preview the effect. The title and background of the slide appears.

4. Press the Page Down key or click the mouse button. The first paragraph (or bullet) appears using the chosen effect.

5. Keep pressing Page Down or clicking until all of the slide's text is onscreen.

6. Press Esc to return to Slide Sorter view.

CUSTOM ANIMATION

If you want to get more detailed with an object's animation, or if you want to animate multimedia objects (like sounds and video on the slide), you must use custom animation. Here's how:

1. In Slide view, display the slide containing the object(s) to animate.

2. Select Slide Show, Custom Animation. The Custom Animation dialog box appears (see Figure 23.3).

3. In the Slide Objects Without Animation list on the Timing tab, click on the object you want to animate.

4. Click the Animate option button. The object disappears from the Slide Objects Without Animation list, and appears in the Animation Order list.

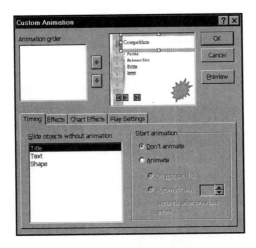

FIGURE 23.3   Use the Custom Animation dialog box to animate objects on a slide using precise settings.

5. Specify when the animation should take place:

   - Leave the On Mouse Click option button selected if you want the animation to happen when you click the mouse (that is, at your command).

   - Click the Automatically option button and specify a number of seconds that should elapse between the action before it and this animation.

6. Repeat steps 3 through 5 until all the objects you want to animate appear in the Animation Order list.

7. Use the up and down arrow buttons to rearrange the items on the Animation Order list if needed. The slide will "build" in the order you specify here.

8. Now it's time to choose the effect itself. Select the object in the Animation Order list for which you want to specify an effect.

9. Click the Effects tab. The Effects controls appear, as shown in Figure 23.4.

10. In the Entry Animation and Sound section, select an effect from the Entry Animation drop-down list (the top one).

11. (Optional) Select a sound to accompany the effect from the Sound drop-down list (the bottom one).

12. Click OK.

13. Use Slide Show view or click the Preview button to test your work.

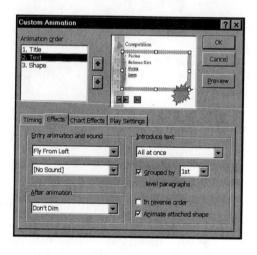

FIGURE 23.4 Use the Effects controls to specify what animation and sound will apply to a slide.

OTHER ANIMATION OPTIONS

As you saw in Figure 23.4, there are many more options in the Custom Animation dialog box for setting up your animation than can be covered here. There simply isn't enough space to delve into them all in this book. Experiment with them, and find your favorite special effects. Here are some ideas to get you started:

- In the Introduce text drop-down list, you can choose to have text appear word-by-word, or even letter-by-letter.

- If you have multiple levels of bullet points in your text, you can animate by a different level other than 1st by choosing it from the Grouped by drop-down list.

- You can build text from the bottom to the top by selecting the In Reverse Order check box.

- You can choose to dim the object after it has been animated. This might come in handy, for instance, if you have a bulleted list in which you want the point you are currently talking about "bright" and the other points "dim."

- As you learned in Lesson 15, you can control how a sound or video clip plays by clicking the Play Settings tab and setting options there. This tab's controls are unavailable unless the selected object is "playable" (i.e. some type of media clip).

In this lesson, you learned how to add timed transitions and animations to your slides. In the next lesson, you will learn how to create speaker's notes pages.

LESSON
24

CREATING SPEAKER'S NOTES

In this lesson, you will learn how to create speaker's notes to help you during the delivery of your presentation.

The problem with many presentations is that the presenter merely flips from one slide to the next, without telling the audience the point or providing an overview that adds meaning. To make your slide show a success, you can put together a set of speaker's notes pages to help you deliver an effective, coherent presentation.

Each notes page is divided into two parts. A small version of the slide appears at the top of the page, and your notes appear below it (see Figure 24.1).

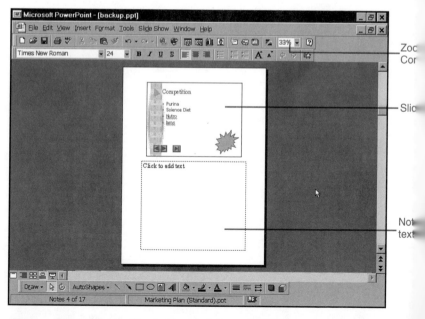

FIGURE 24.1 Example of a speaker's notes page.

CREATING SPEAKER'S NOTES PAGES

You already have the slide part of the speaker's notes pages. All you need to do is type the notes. You type notes in Notes Pages view, as follows:

1. Open the presentation for which you want to create speaker's notes pages.

2. Click the Notes Pages View button at the bottom of the presentation window or select View, Notes Pages. The currently selected slide appears in Notes Pages view, as shown in Figure 24.1.

3. Click on the Notes text box in the lower half of the notes page to select it.

4. To see what you type, open the Zoom Control drop-down list on the Standard toolbar and click on a zoom percentage (refer to Figure 24.1). 100% works well.

5. Type the text that you want to use as notes material for this slide. (You can include reminders, jokes, supporting data, or explanations about how the slide fits in with the presentation's big picture.)

6. Press the Page Up or Page Down key to move to another notes page, and then repeat step 5.

7. Format your text if you want. (For details on how to format text, refer to Lessons 12 and 13.)

Save Your Notes   When typing your notes, don't forget to save your work on a regular basis. Once you save and name your presentation file, saving again is as simple as pressing Ctrl+S.

CHANGING THE SIZE OF THE SLIDE AND TEXT BOX

As explained earlier, each notes page contains two objects: a slide and a text box. You change the size of either object just as you change the size of any object in PowerPoint (see Lesson 16).

1. Click on the slide's picture or text box to select it. (If you click on the text box, a frame appears around it. Click on the frame to display handles.)

2. Move the mouse pointer over one of the object's handles. (Use a corner handle to change both the width and height of the object. Use a side, top, or bottom handle to change only one dimension at a time.)

3. Hold down the mouse button and drag the handle until the object is the size you want.

4. Release the mouse button.

TIP   **Consistent Notes Pages**   To keep the size of the slides and note text boxes consistent on all notes pages, change the size on the Notes Master. The following section explains how to display and work with the Notes Master.

WORKING WITH THE NOTES MASTER

Just as a slide show has a Slide Master that contains the background and layout for all the slides in the presentation, the Notes Master contains the background and layout for all your notes pages. You can use the Notes Master to do the following:

• Add background information (such as the date, time, or page numbers) you want to appear on all the notes pages.

• Add a picture, such as a company logo, that you want to appear on each notes page.

- Move or resize objects on the notes pages.

- Choose a color scheme or background for the slide. (This affects the look of the slide only on the notes pages, not in the presentation itself.)

- Set up the Body Area of the Notes Master to control the general layout and formatting of the text in the notes area of each notes page.

To change the Notes Master, perform the following steps:

1. Select View, Master, Notes Master, or hold down Shift as you click the Notes Pages View button. The Notes Master appears.

2. Change any of the elements in the Notes Master as you would in Slide Master.

In this lesson, you learned how to create speaker's notes pages to help in the delivery of a presentation. In the next lesson, you will learn how to create audience handouts.

CREATING AUDIENCE HANDOUTS

In this lesson, you will learn how to create handouts to distribute to your audience.

HANDOUTS HELP YOUR AUDIENCE

Most presenters move through a presentation fairly quickly, giving the audience little time to filter through all the data on the slides. Because of this, it is often useful to give the audience handouts or copies of the presentation slides. You do this by printing a replica of your slide show on paper, or by printing several slides per page.

PRINTING HANDOUTS

Creating handouts is fairly easy. Choose File, Print and open the Print What drop-down list. You see the Handouts options shown in Figure 25.1. You can choose to print 2, 3, or 6 slides to a page. (For details on how to print, refer to Lesson 7.)

Printing in Black and White   If you don't have a color printer, select the Black & White check box in the Print dialog box. This option formats your output for a one-color printout.

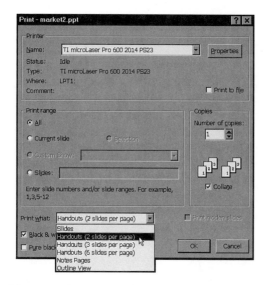

FIGURE 25.1   You can choose to print 2, 3, or 6 slides per page.

DISPLAYING THE HANDOUT MASTER

The Handout Master controls the placement and look of the slides on the audience handouts. The slide image placeholders on the Handout Master show you where you can place slides on a handout. To display the Handout Master, perform the following steps:

1. Select View, Master, Handout Master or hold down the Shift key and click on the Slide Sorter View button. The Handout Master appears, as shown in Figure 25.2.

2. Zoom in so you can see what you're doing: choose a zoom percentage—66% works well—from the Zoom drop-down list on the Standard toolbar (refer to Figure 25.2).

3. Click the 2 per page, 3 per page, or 6 per page button to change to the print layout you want to affect. There are separate Handout Master layouts for each type of printout you can choose in the Print dialog box (see Figure 25.1).

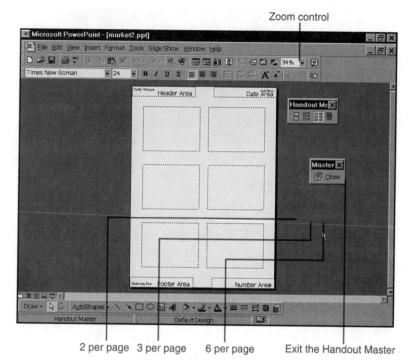

Zoom control

2 per page   3 per page   6 per page   Exit the Handout Master

FIGURE 25.2   The Handout Master.

4. Make any changes to the Handout Master that you want to appear on all handouts. For instance, you might want your company's name and logo, and today's date on each page of the handouts.

5. Click the Close button to exit the Handout Master.

6. Print your handouts, as described earlier in this lesson.

In this lesson, you learned how to create audience handouts to accompany your slide presentation. In the next lesson, you will learn how to check your spelling and find and replace data in all your presentation materials.

OTHER EDITING TOOLS

In this lesson, you will learn how to check your presentation for spelling errors, and to find and replace text in all presentation materials.

CHECKING FOR MISSPELLINGS AND TYPOS

PowerPoint uses a built-in dictionary to spell check your entire presentation, including all slides, outlines, notes and handout pages, and all four master views. To check the spelling in your presentation, perform the following steps:

1. Click the Spelling button on the Standard toolbar (Alternatively, select Tools, Spelling, or press F7.)

2. If there are no misspellings, PowerPoint displays a dialog box saying that the spell check is complete. Click OK to close it.

3. If a misspelling is found, the Spelling dialog box appears displaying the first questionable word with all the options for handling it (see Figure 26.1).

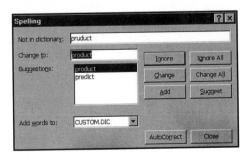

FIGURE 26.1 The Spelling dialog box displays the questionable word and suggests corrections.

4. For the word that the spell checker found, select one of these options:

- Ignore to skip only this occurrence of the word.

- Ignore All to ignore every occurrence of the word.

- Change to replace only this occurrence of the word with the word in the Change To box. (You can type a correction in the Change To box or select a correct spelling from the Suggestions list.)

- Change All to replace every occurrence of the word with the word in the Change To box. (To insert an entry in the Change To box, type it, or select an entry from the Suggestions list.)

- Add to add the word to the dictionary, so the spell checker will not question it again.

- Suggest to display a list of suggested words. You can select a word from the Add words to drop-down list to insert it in the Change To box.

- AutoCorrect to add the misspelled word to the AutoCorrect list, with the word that appears in the Change To box as its correction. From then on, PowerPoint will automatically correct that misspelling if you make it again.

- Close to close the Spelling dialog box.

5. Repeat step 3 until the spell checker finishes checking the presentation. When the spell checker finishes, a dialog box appears to tell you that spell check is complete.

6. Click OK.

EDITING THE AUTOCORRECT LIST

There are certain misspellings that many people commonly make, such as transposing letters ("teh" instead of "the") and leaving out letters or apostrophes ("ther" or "youre"). AutoCorrect can identify and correct these common errors for you automatically. And, as you saw in the Spelling dialog box (see Figure 26.1), you can add your own common errors to the list, too.

To view and make changes to the list of AutoCorrected words, follow these steps. Choose Tools, AutoCorrect. The AutoCorrect dialog box opens (see Figure 26.2).

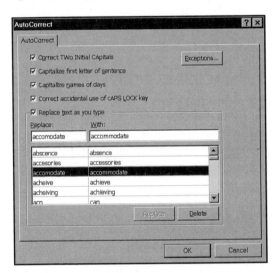

FIGURE 26.2 You can edit the list of AutoCorrected words from this dialog box.

From here, you can do any of the following:

- (Optional) Deselect any of the check boxes at the top of the dialog box to turn off any AutoCorrect features you don't want to use.

- To add a correction to the list, type the misspelling in the Replace text box and the correction in the With text box, and click the Add button.

- To remove a correction from the list, scroll through the list to find it, highlight it, and click the Delete button.

- To make a change to a correction, highlight it, make the change in the Replace or With text boxes, and click the Replace button. When you're finished making changes to the AutoCorrect list, click OK.

TIP

Why Would I Delete an AutoCorrection? In most cases, you will want to leave all the check boxes marked and the corrections in place on the list. However, sometimes a special situation requires you to turn off a correction. For instance, my publisher's editors use (c) to indicate a heading, so I had to delete the AutoCorrect entry that changed (c) to a copyright symbol.

FINDING AND REPLACING TEXT

If you want to find a particular word or phrase in your presentation, but you can't remember where it is, you can have PowerPoint find the word or phrase for you. You can also have PowerPoint search for a word or phrase and replace one or all instances of the word or phrase.

To search for specific text, perform the following steps:

1. Choose Edit, Find, or press Ctrl+F. The Find dialog box appears (see Figure 26.3).

FIGURE 26.3   Use the Find dialog box to find all occurrences of a particular word or phrase.

2. In the Find What text box, type the word or phrase you want to search for in the text.

3. (Optional) Select either or both of the following options:

   • Match Case finds text that matches the capitalization in the Find What text box. For example, if you type Widget, the search skips widget.

- Find Whole Words Only skips any occurrences of the text that appear in a part of another word. For example, if you type book, the search skips bookkeeper.

4. Click the Find Next button. PowerPoint finds next occurrence of the word and highlights it.

Editing and Formatting Text To edit or format text, simply perform the operation as you would under normal circumstances. The Find dialog box remains on-screen as you work.

5. When you've found all occurrences, PowerPoint displays a message to that effect. Click OK to close the message. To close the Find dialog box before you have found all occurrences, click on the Close button.

Quick Jump to Replace If you start out using Find and then realize that you want to replace the found word with something else, just click the Replace button in the Find dialog box to jump to the Replace dialog box explained in the following steps.

To replace a word or phrase with another word or phrase, perform the following steps:

1. Choose Edit, Replace, or press Ctrl+H. The Replace dialog box appears, as shown in Figure 26.4.

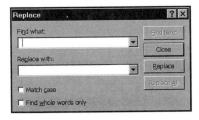

FIGURE 26.4 The Replace dialog box.

2. In the Find What text box, type the word or phrase you want to search for.

3. In the Replace With text box, type the word or phrase you want to use as the replacement.

4. (Optional) Select either or both of the following options:

   • Match Case finds text that matches the capitalization in the Find What text box.

   • Find Whole Words Only skips any occurrences of the text that are a part of another word.

5. Click the Find Next button to find the first occurrence of the word.

6. If PowerPoint finds the text, click on one of the following buttons:

   • Replace replaces one occurrence of the Find What text with the Replace With text.

   • Replace All replaces all occurrences of the Find What text (throughout your presentation) with the Replace With text.

   • Find Next skips the current occurrence of the Find What text and moves to the next occurrence.

7. When PowerPoint has found and replaced all occurrences, a message appears to that effect. Click OK to close it. Or, if you are finished replacing text before PowerPoint comes to the last occurrence, click on the Close button.

In this lesson, you learned how to check your presentation for misspelled words and typos, and how to find and replace words and phrases. In the next lesson, you'll learn how to import and export data in PowerPoint.

EXCHANGING DATA

In this lesson, you will learn how to import and export PowerPoint data so you can use parts of your presentations in other programs. You'll also learn how to use data from other programs in your presentations and share data with other people.

IMPORTING SLIDES AND PRESENTATIONS

PowerPoint's outline view provides a convenient way for you to type in information for your slides, but you may prefer to work in another program instead, such as your word processor. Or, you may already have the entire presentation typed into another program.

You can import text as an entirely new presentation, or you can insert text into an existing presentation.

OPENING A PRESENTATION CREATED IN ANOTHER PROGRAM

PowerPoint can open presentations created in almost any other presentation graphics program, such as Harvard Graphics or Lotus Freelance. The conversion may be imperfect, and you may have to do some reformatting, but the essential data converts. To open a presentation from another program, follow these steps:

1. Choose File, Open. The File Open dialog box appears.

2. Open the Files of Type drop-down list and choose the type of presentation you plan to import (if you know). (See Figure 27.1.) Or, if you don't know, choose All Files Types.

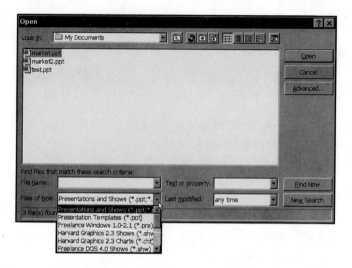

FIGURE 27.1 You can open several types of files besides PowerPoint.

3. Select the presentation file, and click Open.

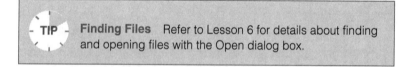

- **TIP** **Finding Files** Refer to Lesson 6 for details about finding and opening files with the Open dialog box.

CREATING A NEW PRESENTATION FROM A TEXT OUTLINE

You are not limited to other presentation programs' files to open; you can open almost any text file in a new PowerPoint file. Of course, after you import, you have to do some reformatting of the file. Follow the same steps as for importing a presentation file from another presentation program, except choose All Outlines as the file type.

INSERTING INDIVIDUAL SLIDES FROM OTHER PRESENTATIONS

PowerPoint can import individual slides not only from other PowerPoint presentations, but from presentations created in other programs, too, like Harvard Graphics. See "Adding Slides from Another Presentation" in Lesson 9 for a refresher course in how to insert slides into a presentation.

USING DATA FROM POWERPOINT IN OTHER PROGRAMS

After you've spent a lot of time creating a PowerPoint presentation, you might want to use some of the data in another program. For example, you might want to base a Microsoft Word report on a PowerPoint presentation. There are several ways to transfer data from PowerPoint to another program.

EXPORTING A PRESENTATION

If you need to use your PowerPoint presentation in another program, you can save an entire presentation as a different file type. PowerPoint does not export files to as many formats as it can import; for instance, you cannot directly save your PowerPoint presentation as a Harvard Graphics file. However, you can export the data from the presentation in a more generic form, such as RTF (Rich Text Format), that you can import to other graphics programs.

Follow these steps to save a presentation file in a different format:

1. Choose File, Save As. The File Save dialog box appears.

2. Open the Save as Type drop-down list and choose the file type in which you wish to save your presentation (see Figure 27.2).

3. Type a name for the new version of the presentation in the File name box.

4. Click Save.

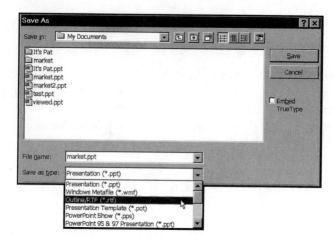

FIGURE 27.2 You can save your PowerPoint presentation in several other formats.

TRANSFERRING PARTS OF A PRESENTATION TO ANOTHER PROGRAM

Even though you can't export individual slides from PowerPoint, you can take advantage of the Windows Clipboard to transfer bits of a presentation to other programs. To use the Clipboard, follow these steps:

1. Select the objects in PowerPoint that you want to use in another program.

 2. Click the Copy button or choose Edit, Copy.

3. Open the other program and the document into which you want to paste the PowerPoint pieces.

 4. Click the Paste button or choose Edit, Paste.

SHARING YOUR PRESENTATION WITH OTHER PEOPLE

If you work in a team environment, you may need to share your in progress PowerPoint work with other people, to get their input on your work. One of the best ways is to route it to them using your e-mail.

Just open the presentation; select File, Send To and select either Mail Recipient or Routing Recipient. Depending on your mail system, different dialog boxes or screens appear asking you for the mailing information. Fill in the dialog boxes that appear, and the file is on its way via your local area network.

Mail versus Routing   When you mail a file to many recipients, they all receive the same file at once. In contrast, when you route to many recipients, they receive it one person at a time. When one person is finished, he routes it to the next person, and it returns to you after the last person has seen it. Routing works well if you expect each recipient to make changes to the file that need to be incorporated into your final draft.

Unfortunately, PowerPoint does not support revision marks, so you can't easily tell what changes have been made to your presentation as it was being routed around. That's why it's important to save a copy of the original file you routed, in case someone makes changes to it that you don't want.

If you don't want any of the routing recipients to be able to make changes to your presentation, you can make the file read-only before you send it. Here's how:

1. Save the file in PowerPoint (see Lesson 6).

2. Exit PowerPoint and open Windows Explorer (Start, Programs, Windows Explorer).

3. Right-click on the saved file, and select Properties from the shortcut menu that appears.

4. In the file's Properties dialog box, select the Read-Only check box.

5. Go back into PowerPoint and reopen the file.

6. Use the File, Send To command to send or route the file to your recipients. They will be able to view the file, but not make changes.

In this lesson, you learned how to import and export PowerPoint presentations and how to mail or route a file to other users. In the next lesson, you'll learn how to create dynamic links between PowerPoint and other programs.

OBJECT LINKING AND EMBEDDING

28

In this lesson, you'll learn about Object Linking and Embedding (OLE), and you'll find out how to link data from other programs to your PowerPoint presentation.

WHAT IS OLE?

Object Linking and Embedding, or OLE, is a way to ensure that your documents are always up-to-date. When you import or paste a graphic, chart, or other object into a presentation, the pasted piece is "dead"—that is, it never changes. In contrast, when you link an object to a presentation, the object stays "alive." When you open and edit it in its native program, PowerPoint reflects those changes in its copy of the object.

LINKING OR EMBEDDING: WHAT'S THE DIFFERENCE?

Linking and embedding are actually two different things, although few people really understand the difference.

Embedding is what happens whenever you insert an object into a presentation using Insert, Object. PowerPoint places the object in the presentation, and you double-click on it to open its native program and edit the object on-the-spot.

Linking is everything that embedding is, plus more. Just like with embedding, you double-click on the file to edit it. With a linked file, however, you make changes to that file outside of Power-Point, and the copy in the PowerPoint presentation updates automatically. How? When PowerPoint opens the presentation, it retrieves each linked object again, getting the freshest copy of the object.

LINKING A FILE TO A PRESENTATION

If you have a file in another program (for instance, a graphic in Windows Paint program), you can link it to a PowerPoint presentation. To link the file to your presentation, follow these steps:

1. Display the slide onto which you want to place the object.

2. Choose Insert, Object. The Insert Object dialog box appears.

3. Click Create from File. The dialog box changes, as shown in Figure 28.1.

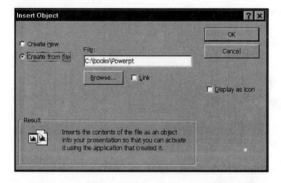

FIGURE 28.1   The Insert Object dialog box enables you to link an object.

4. Type the complete path and file name of the file you want to link, or click the Browse button to use a dialog box to find it.

5. Select the Link check box. This is important! It makes the difference between linking and merely embedding.

6. Click OK.

EMBEDDING AN OBJECT IN A PRESENTATION

With linking, a file has to already exist. You can't create a file on-the-spot and then link it.

With embedding, you have this added flexibility. You can either embed an existing file, or create and embed a new one by opening the native program right there in PowerPoint.

To embed an existing file, just follow the steps for linking in the previous section, but do not select the Link check box. To create a new file and embed it, perform the following steps:

1. Display the slide onto which you want to place the object.

2. Choose Insert, Object. The Insert Object dialog box appears.

3. Click Create New. You see the options shown in Figure 28.2.

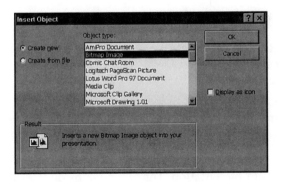

FIGURE 28.2   Use these options to create a new file and embed it.

4. Choose an object type, based on the program you are using to create the object. For instance, you choose Paintbrush Picture to embed a graphics file.

5. Click OK. A small box in the center of the slide opens, and the controls for that program appear. You create your new object in that box (see Figure 28.3).

These are Paint menus   I drew these shapes with Paint   Here is my PowerPoint slide

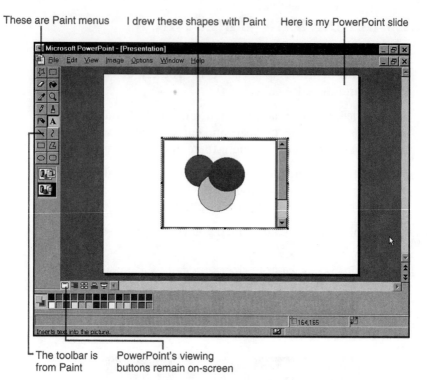

The toolbar is   PowerPoint's viewing
from Paint   buttons remain on-screen

FIGURE 28.3 You can create a graphic to embed in your PowerPoint slide.

6. Create the new file using the program. (Refer to the program's documentation for instructions on how to use that program.)

7. Click anywhere outside the box to return to your PowerPoint presentation. The box remains on the slide, and you can move the box around like any other object.

8. If you want to edit the object, just double-click on it.

In this lesson, you learned to link and embed objects in your presentation. In the next lesson, you'll learn about using PowerPoint presentations on the Internet.

USING POWERPOINT ON THE INTERNET

In this lesson, you'll learn how PowerPoint makes it easy to publish your presentations on the World Wide Web or your corporate intranet.

The World Wide Web is the most popular and graphical component of the Internet, a worldwide network of computers. Many businesses maintain Web sites containing information about their products and services for public reading. Still other businesses maintain an internal version of the Web that's strictly for employee use, and they use the company's local area network to make it available to its staff. These are called *intranets*.

Sooner or later, you may be asked to prepare a PowerPoint presentation for use on a Web site or an intranet. Don't panic! It's simpler than it sounds.

WEB PRESENTATION DESIGNS

You may have noticed back in Lesson 2, when you created a new presentation, that some of the presentation design templates had (Online) in their names. Those templates are made especially for creating presentations that will be displayed online (on the Web or an intranet), and contain special controls toward that end. For instance, the presentation shown in Figure 29.1 came ready-made with navigation buttons at the bottom of each slide—you don't have to create these buttons manually (as in Lesson 22). PowerPoint provides an online version of almost every template it ships with.

Web navigation buttons are part of this template.

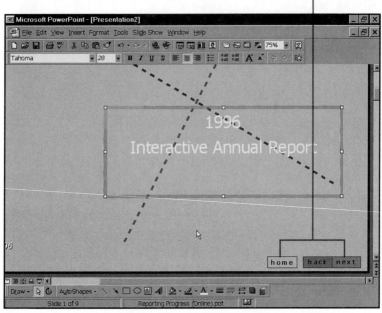

FIGURE 29.1   Basing your presentation on one of the Internet-based presentation design templates can give you a big head start.

ADDING URL HYPERLINKS

Remember back in Lesson 22, when we added action buttons to a slide? The action buttons moved us from slide to slide in the presentation. You can also assign links to Web addresses (URLs) to a button. For instance, you might have a button that takes you to your company's home page (the top page at their Internet site) at the bottom of every slide.

Let's say you've started a new presentation based on a design template for online use. It already has buttons for Home, Previous, and Next. You want to set the Home button to jump to your Web site's home page when clicked (**http://www.mysite.com**). Perform the following steps:

1. In Slide view, click on the Home button, so selection handles appear around it.

No Selection Handles! If you click on the button and it doesn't appear to be selected, the button may actually be on the Slide Master. Choose View, Masters, Slide Master or hold down Shift and click on the Slide View button, and try clicking on the button there instead.

2. Choose Slide Show, Action Settings. The Action Settings dialog box appears.

3. Click the Hyperlink To button.

4. Open the Hyperlink To drop-down list and select URL.

5. In the dialog box that appears, type the URL you want to link to (for example, **http://www.mcp.com**). See Figure 29.2.

6. Click OK twice to close both dialog boxes.

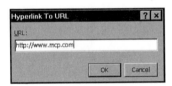

FIGURE 29.2 Enter the URL that you want to hyperlink to when the user clicks the button.

Now it's time to test your hyperlink. View the slide in Slide Show view, and click on the button with your mouse. Your Web browser should start and the selected URL should load in it.

> **Make Your Own Buttons**   You don't have to rely on the
> template creating the buttons for you; you can create your
> **TIP**   own action buttons, as you learned in Lesson 22. To
> create a custom button and type text on it, select the
> blank button and then type in it after you create it.

SAVING A PRESENTATION IN HTML FORMAT

A new feature in PowerPoint 97 is the ability to save files in HTML format. This comes in very handy because it turns your presentations into documents that can be displayed in any Web browser program, without any help from the PowerPoint application. Since all World Wide Web users have Web browser programs, no one need miss out on your presentation.

The downside, of course, is that the translation is not perfect. Your presentation may not look exactly the same in HTML format as it did in PowerPoint itself. But all the text will be there, and some of the formatting.

1. Choose File, Save As HTML. The Save As HTML Wizard opens to walk you through the process. Click Next to begin.

2. Choose an existing layout from the Load Existing Layout list, or leave the New Layout button selected. (You don't have any choice if you haven't created any layouts yet; you must use New Layout.) Then click Next.

3. Choose a page style: Standard or Browser Frames, and then click Next.

    -   **Standard** is a simple one-pane view that will display correctly on almost all browsers.

    -   **Browser Frames** is fancier but might not display correctly unless the user viewing the presentation has a recent version of Netscape or Internet Explorer.

4. Choose a graphic type for your graphics to be exported to and click Next to continue.

   - GIF and JPEG are both equally acceptable standard formats for graphics. GIF is more common, but JPEG is smaller and more recognized on the Internet. These formats do not support animation, so any animation you have assigned will be lost.

   - PowerPoint Animation format requires users to download a special PowerPoint viewer, but it ensures that your animations and effects will remain true to your original planning.

5. Choose a screen size that your presentation should be optimized for display on. 640×480 has long been the standard in VGA systems, but lately many people have been switching to 800×600 resolutions. Then click Next.

6. Where prompted, enter your e-mail address and/or your Web page address. These will be available to your users as they view your presentation. Then click Next.

7. Next you're asked about colors. Click Use Browser Colors to go with the users' defaults, or click Custom Colors and choose your own. Then click Next to continue.

8. Click on the option button next to the button style you want, and then click Next.

9. Choose a Navigation button placement. If you want to include your slide notes in the presentation, click the Include slide notes in pages check box. Then click Next.

10. In the Create HTML Folder In text box, enter the folder in which you want to store your converted HTML documents. The default is \My Documents. Then click Next.

11. Click the Finish button to complete the process.

   A dialog box appears asking for a name for these settings, in case you want to reuse them in the future. Enter a name and click Save. From now on, that name will be

available at step 2 in the list of layouts. If you don't want
to save the settings, click Don't Save.

12. Wait for PowerPoint to save the file. When you see the
message "The presentation was successfully saved as
HTML," click OK.

After you have saved a presentation in HTML format, you must
copy it to the server on which you want to make it available. If
you use a modem to connect to an Internet service provider,
establish your modem connection and use an FTP program to
upload the files to the appropriate directory on the server. If you
use a LAN or intranet, consult your system administrator to find
out where to put the files.

PowerPoint Viewers

There are two ways to provide PowerPoint content to Web users.
One is to save the presentation in a pure HTML format. (That's
what you did in the preceding steps, unless you chose PowerPoint
Animation format in step 4.) The PowerPoint file becomes a
generic HTML file that is viewable in almost any Web browser.
The person viewing it does not need to have PowerPoint installed
on their computer.

The other way is to simply copy the PowerPoint presentation in
its native .ppt format to the Web server and let the readers access
it as a PowerPoint presentation. This is good because it preserves
all your animations and transitions, but it requires that all your
readers have a copy of PowerPoint installed.

A partial solution for this situation is to provide your audience
with a PowerPoint viewer program. This program is a "runtime"
version of PowerPoint, containing just enough of the right stuff to
view your presentation on-screen. The reader can't make any
changes to the presentation; it's like being permanently in Slide
Show view.

You can get the PowerPoint viewer directly from Microsoft's Web
site. Just visit **http://www.microsoft.com/mspowerpoint/
Internet/Viewer/default.htm**. It's free and freely distributed,
so you can provide a copy to all your users on your intranet, or

you can provide a link to the viewer on your company's Web site
so that anyone who doesn't yet have the viewer can download it
directly from Microsoft. After users have the PowerPoint viewer,
and have downloaded your presentation file from the Web, they
can run the viewer like any program and load the presentation
file into it to view it. Figure 29.3 shows a presentation being
loaded for viewing in the PowerPoint viewer.

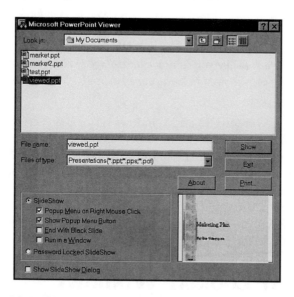

FIGURE 29.3   You can't give everyone a copy of PowerPoint, but
it's perfectly legal to give everyone the PowerPoint viewer.

 TIP   **A PowerPoint Plug-In**   If you use Netscape as your
primary Web browser, you can download a variety of
plug-ins for it that enable you to view PowerPoint presentations without leaving the Netscape window.

In this lesson, you learned about PowerPoint's capabilities in
helping you present your slides on the Web.

THE WINDOWS PRIMER

Windows 95 and Windows NT are graphical operating systems that make your computer easy to use by providing menus and pictures from which you select. Before you can take advantage of either operating system, however, you need to learn some basics that apply to both of them.

Fortunately, Windows 95 and Windows NT operate very much alike. (In fact, they're so similar I'll refer to them both just as Windows throughout the remainder of this appendix.) If the figures you see in this primer don't look exactly like what's on your screen, don't sweat it. Some slight variation may occur depending on your setup, the applications you use, and whether you're on a network. Rest assured, however, that the basic information presented here applies no matter what your setup might be.

A FIRST LOOK AT WINDOWS

You don't really have to start Windows because it starts automatically when you turn on your PC. After the initial startup screens, you arrive at a screen something like the one shown in Figure A.1.

PARTS OF THE SCREEN

As you can see, the Windows screen contains a lot of special elements and controls. Here's a brief summary of those elements:

- The Desktop consists of the background and icons that represent programs, tools, and other elements.

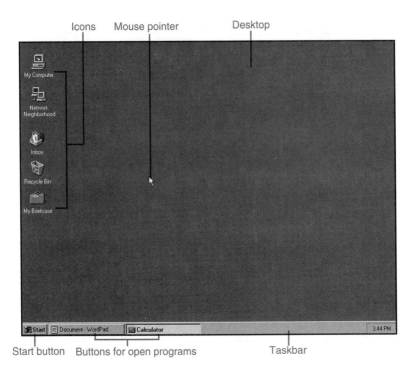

Icons   Mouse pointer   Desktop

Start button   Buttons for open programs   Taskbar

FIGURE A.1   **The Windows screen.**

- The Taskbar shows a button for each open window and program. You can switch between open windows and programs by clicking the taskbar button that represents the program you want. (The program you are currently working in is highlighted in the taskbar.)

- The Start button opens a menu from which you can start programs, get help, and find files. To use it, click the Start button, and then point or click to make a selection from each successive menu that appears. (When you point to a selection that has a right-pointing arrow beside it, a secondary—or cascading—menu appears.)

- The icons that appear on your desktop give you access to certain programs and computer components. You open an icon by double-clicking it. (An open icon displays a window containing programs, files, or other items.)

- The mouse pointer moves around the screen in relation to your movement of the mouse. You use the mouse pointer to select what you want to work with.

You'll learn more about these elements as you work through the rest of this Windows primer.

TIP **Also Appearing: Microsoft Office** If your computer has Microsoft Office installed on it, the Office Shortcuts toolbar also appears on-screen. It's a series of little pictures strung together horizontally that represent Office programs. Hold the mouse over a picture (icon) to see what it does; click it to launch the program. See your Microsoft Office documentation to learn more.

You may have some other icons on your desktop (representing networks, folders, printers, files, and so on) depending upon what options you chose during initial setup. Double-click an icon to view the items it contains.

Using a Mouse

To work most efficiently in Windows, you need a mouse. You will perform the following mouse actions as you work:

- **Point** To position the mouse so that the on-screen pointer touches an item.

- **Click** To press and release the left mouse button once. Clicking an item usually selects it. Except when you're told to do otherwise (for example to right-click), you always use the left mouse button.

TIP **Southpaw Strategy** You can reverse these mouse button actions if you want to use the mouse left-handed. To do so, click Start, Settings, Control Panel, and Mouse. Then click the Buttons tab of the Control Panel dialog box and choose Left-handed.

- **Double-click**   To press and release the left mouse button twice quickly. Double-clicking usually activates an item or opens a window, folder, or program. (Double-clicking may take some practice because the speed needs to be just right. To change the speed so it better matches your "clicking style," choose Start, Settings, Control Panel, and Mouse. Then click the Buttons tab of the Mouse Properties dialog box and adjust the double-clicking speed so that it's just right for you.

- **Drag**   To place the mouse pointer over the element you want to move, press and hold down the left mouse button, and then move the mouse to a new location. You might drag to move a window, dialog box, or file from one location to another. Except when you're told to do otherwise (for example to right-drag), you drag with the left mouse button.

- **Right-click**   To click with the right mouse button. Right-clicking usually displays a shortcut (or pop-up) menu from which you can choose common commands.

CONTROLLING A WINDOW WITH THE MOUSE

Ever wonder why the program is called "Windows"? Well, Windows operating systems section off the desktop into rectangular work areas called *windows*. These windows are used for particular purposes, such as running a program, displaying options or lists, and so on. Each window has common features used to manipulate the window. Figure A.2 shows how you can use the mouse to control your windows.

Click to shrink the window   Click to expand the window   Click to close
to a button on the taskbar.   to fill the entire screen.   the window.

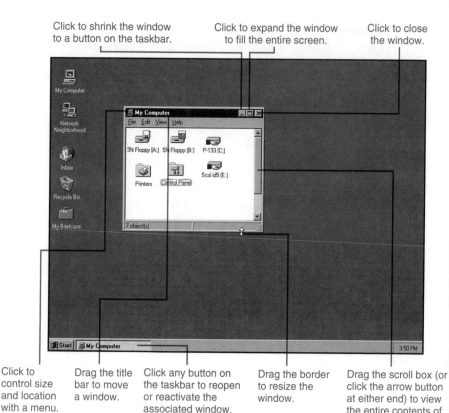

Click to   Drag the title   Click any button on   Drag the border   Drag the scroll box (or
control size   bar to move   the taskbar to reopen to resize the   click the arrow button
and location   a window.   or reactivate the   window.   at either end) to view
with a menu.   associated window.   the entire contents of
                                                                                the window.

FIGURE A.2   Use your mouse to control and manipulate windows.

TIP

Scrolling for Information   If your window contains more
information than it can display, scroll bars appear on the
bottom and/or right edges of the window. To move
through the window, click an arrow button at either end of
a scroll bar or drag the scroll box in the direction you want
to move.

If you're using the professional version of Office 97, you'll
also have enhanced scrolling available via your
"Intellimouse"—a new mouse by Microsoft that includes a
scrolling wheel. Using this mouse is described in all Que
books that cover Microsoft Office 97 and its individual
applications.

GETTING HELP

Windows comes with a great online Help system. To access it, click the Start button and then click Help. Figure A.3 shows the main Help window with the Contents tab displayed.

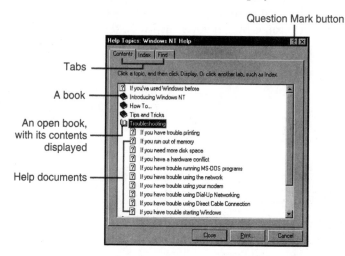

Question Mark button

Tabs

A book

An open book, with its contents displayed

Help documents

FIGURE A.3　Windows offers several kinds of help.

As you can see here, the Help box contains three tabs (Contents, Index, and Find), each of which provides you with a different type of help. To move to a tab, just click it.

Here's how to use each tab:

- **Contents**　Double-click any book to open it and see its sub-books and documents. Double-click a sub-book or document to open it and read the Help topic.

- **Index**　When you click this tab, Windows asks you for more information on what you're looking for. Type the word you want to look up, and the Index list scrolls to that part of the alphabetical listing. When you see the topic that you want to read in the list, double-click it.

- **Find**　The first time you click this tab, Windows tells you it needs to create a list. Click Next and then Finish to allow this. When Windows finishes, it asks you to type the word you want to find in the top text box. Then click a word in the middle box to narrow the search. And finally, review the list of Help topics at the bottom and double-click the one you want to read.

When you finish reading about a document, click Help Topics to return to the main Help screen, or click Back to return to the previous Help topic. When you finish with the Help system itself, click the window's Close (X) button to exit.

Another Way to Get Help In the upper-right corner of the Help window, you should see a question mark next to the Close button. This is (surprise!) the Question Mark button. Whenever you see this button (it appears in other windows besides the Help window), you can click it to change your mouse pointer to a combined arrow-and-question mark. You can then point at any element in the window for a quick "pop-up" description of that element.

Some applications or application suites (such as Microsoft Office 97) also offer online help. You can learn more about using online help by reading the application's documentation or any Que book that covers the application.

STARTING A PROGRAM

Of the many possible ways to start a program, this is the simplest:

1. Click the Start button.

2. Point to Programs.

3. Click the group that contains the program you want to start (such as Accessories).

4. Click the program you want to start (such as Notepad).

Figure A.4 shows the series of menus you would go through to start the Notepad application (as suggested in these steps).

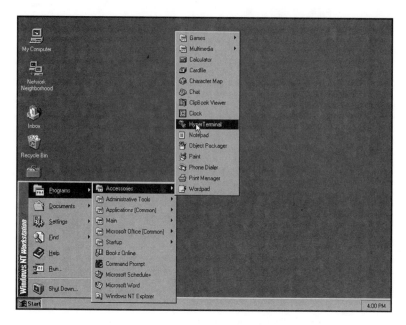

FIGURE A.4 Work through the Start menu and its successive submenus until you find the program you want to start.

Here are a few more ways you can start a program in Windows:

- Open a document that you created in that program. The program automatically opens when the document opens. For example, double-click the My Computer icon on the desktop, find the icon of the document you want to open, and then double-click a document file.

- (Optional) Open a document you created in that program by clicking the Start button, pointing to Programs, and then clicking Windows Explorer. The Windows Explorer window opens; it looks very similar to the File Manager window you've worked with in Windows 3.1. Locate the directory (or "folder" in Windows 95/NT 4.0 terminology) and double-click the file name. The document opens in the program in which it was created.

- Click the Start button, point to Documents, and select a recently used document from the Documents submenu.

Windows immediately starts the program in which you created the file and opens the file.

- If you created a shortcut to the program, you can start the program by double-clicking its shortcut icon on the desktop.

What's a Shortcut?   Shortcut icons are links to other files. When you use a shortcut, Windows simply follows the link back to the original file. If you find that you use any document or program frequently, you might consider creating a desktop shortcut for it. To do so, just use the right mouse button to drag an object out of Windows Explorer or My Computer and onto the desktop. In the shortcut menu that appears, select Create Shortcut(s) Here.

USING MENUS

Almost every Windows program has a menu bar that contains menus. The menu names appear in a row across the top of the screen. To open a menu, click its name (after you click anywhere in the menu bar, you need only point to a menu name to produce the drop-down menu). The menu drops down, displaying its commands (as shown in Figure A.5). To select a command, you simply click it.

Usually, when you select a command, Windows executes the command immediately. But you need to keep in mind the following exceptions to that rule:

- If the command name is gray (instead of black), the command is unavailable at the moment, and you cannot choose it.

- If the command name is followed by an arrow (as the selections on the Start menu are), selecting the command causes another menu to appear, from which you must make another selection.

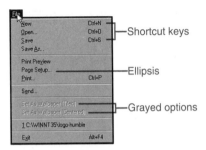

FIGURE A.5 A menu lists various commands you can perform.

- If the command is followed by an ellipsis (...), selecting it will cause a dialog box to appear. You'll learn about dialog boxes later in this primer.

TIP **Shortcut Keys** Key names appear after some command names (for example, Ctrl+O appears to the right of the Open command, and Ctrl+S appears next to the Save command). These are shortcut keys, and you can use them to perform the command without opening the menu. You should also note that some menu names and commands have one letter underlined. By pressing Alt+the underlined letter in a menu name, you can open the menu; by pressing the underlined letter in a command name, you can select that command from the open menu.

USING SHORTCUT MENUS

A fairly new feature in Windows is the shortcut or pop-up menu. Right-click any object (any icon, screen element, file, or folder), and a shortcut menu like the one shown in Figure A.6 appears. The shortcut menu contains commands that apply only to the selected object. Click any command to select it, or click outside the menu to cancel it.

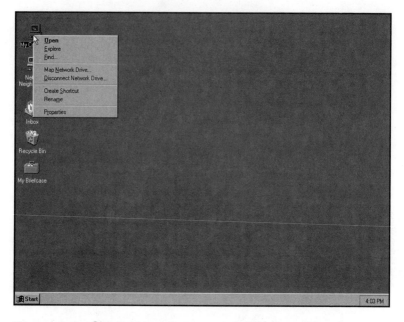

Figure A.6 Shortcut menus are new in Windows 95 and Windows NT 4.0.

Navigating Dialog Boxes

A dialog box is Windows way of requesting additional information or giving you information. For example, if you choose Print from the File menu of the WordPad application, you see a dialog box something like the one shown in Figure A.7. (The options it displays will vary from system to system.)

Each dialog box contains one or more of the following elements:

- List boxes display available choices. Click any item in the list to select it. If the entire list is not visible, use the scroll bar to see additional choices.

- Drop-down lists are similar to list boxes, but only one item in the list is shown. To see the rest of the list, click the drop-down arrow (to the right of the list box), and then click an item to select it.

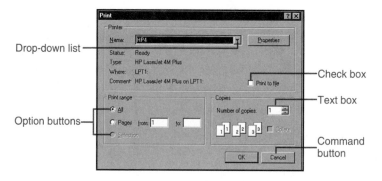

Drop-down list
Check box
Text box
Option buttons
Command button

FIGURE A.7 A dialog box often requests additional information.

- Text boxes enable you to type an entry. Just click inside the text box and type. Text boxes that are designed to hold numbers usually have up and down arrow buttons (called increment buttons) that let you bump the number up and down.

- Check boxes enable you to turn individual options on or off by clicking them. (A check mark or "X" appears when an option is on.) Each check box is an independent unit that doesn't affect other check boxes.

- Option buttons are like check boxes, except that option buttons appear in groups and you can select only one. When you select an option button, the program automatically deselects whichever one was previously selected. Click a button to activate it, and a black bullet appears inside of the white option circle.

- Command buttons perform an action, such as executing the options you set (OK), canceling the options (Cancel), closing the dialog box, or opening another dialog box. To select a command button, click it.

- Tabs bring up additional "pages" of options you can choose. Click a tab to activate it. (See the section on online help for more information on tabs.)

FROM HERE

If you need more help with Windows, you might want to pick up one of these books:

The Complete Idiot's Guide to Windows 95 by Paul McFedries

Easy Windows 95 by Sue Plumley

The Big Basics Book of Windows 95 by Shelley O'Hara, Jennifer Fulton, and Ed Guilford

Using Windows 95 by Ed Bott

The Complete Idiot's Guide to Windows NT 4.0 Workstation by Paul McFedries

Using Windows NT 4.0 Workstation by Ed Bott

INDEX